THE AMERICAN FARM

A PHOTOGRAPHIC HISTORY

by Maisie Conrat and Richard Conrat

California Historical Society, San Francisco / Houghton Mifflin Company, Boston   1977

DC2 H

A portion of this book has appeared in *Smithsonian*.

Library of Congress Cataloging in Publication Data

Conrat, Maisie.
   The American farm.

   Bibliography: p
   1. Agriculture—United States—History. 2. Agricul-
ture—United States—Pictorial works. I. Conrat,
Richard, joint author. II. Title.
S441.C75   338.1'0973   76-55413
ISBN 0-395-25105-2   ISBN 0-395-25359-4 pbk.

Printed in the United States of America

H,M 10 9 8 7 6 5 4 3 2 1

Contents

Introduction

American agriculture has had many faces. Its history, in reality, is not one story, but many. This book is an attempt to create a photographic portrait of the American farm in all its diverse aspects: Not only the traditional yeoman farmer plowing and sowing his own fields, but also the long row of slave cabins on a Georgia cotton plantation. Not only the pioneer family posed proudly before their newly acquired homestead, but also the gang of Asian farmworkers laboring on one of California's vast estates. Not only the glory of an abundant North Dakota wheat harvest, but also the human tragedy embodied in the image of a deserted farmhouse.

In addition, this book is concerned with the changing nature of agriculture in the United States as it developed from a simple, self-sufficing way of life, absorbing the energies of over 90 percent of the nation's citizens, into a highly technical and mechanized industry, requiring large inputs of capital and employing less than 5 percent of the population. This great transformation involved not only a revolution in agricultural technology and methods — a transition from ox-power to four-wheel-drive tractors, from diversified farming to large-scale specialized production — it also involved a change in popular attitudes toward the occupation of farming.

At the time of the Revolution, when the vast majority of Americans drew their living from the land, it was common to think of farming as a social and cultural institution, rather than simply as an economic enterprise. Many statesmen and intellectuals of the period believed that the farmer was imbued with a natural virtue through his close contact with the earth, and that a large farming population together with a wide distribution of land was the soundest basis upon which to build a democratic society. Agriculture, it was believed, yielded not only crops, but also a spiritual and cultural harvest.

As traditional, self-sufficing farming was gradually replaced by production for the market, new attitudes toward agriculture began to emerge. Increasingly the cultivation of the soil was viewed chiefly as a way of making money and only secondarily as a way of life. By the latter part of the nineteenth century, specialized, commercial agriculture had become widespread throughout the United States, and farming was coming to be regarded more and more as a purely business venture. In some regions of the country, agriculture had become commercially oriented at an even earlier time. The slave plantations of the South were a dramatic example of early market-directed, capitalistic agriculture.

The American environment was highly conducive to the development of an intensely commercial and speculative attitude toward farming. The existence of an immense frontier tended to make the nation's farm population restless and opportunistic. The abundance of cheap western lands induced many pioneer farmers to be land exploiters, rather than cultivators of the soil. Urbanization and industrialization created expanding markets for the farmer's produce and awakened dreams of growing rich with a few bonanza harvests. Like other segments of the nation's economy, agriculture became obsessed with bigness and machinery and moneymaking.

As Americans ceased to be an agricultural people, the idea that the well-being of society was dependent upon a large rural population began to lose its meaning, together with the belief that there was some special value in close contact with nature. As the United States developed into a leading industrial nation, farming came to be regarded as just another of the country's many important industries.

It was an industry with many economic classes. On the top were the farmers with capital who could afford to expand their operations and purchase the latest machinery. On the bottom were the farm laborers, the sharecroppers, the tenants, the heavily mortgaged small farmers who had more in common with underpaid factory workers than with upper-class or capitalist farmers. Agriculture became a highly competitive business, and many small farmers found it increasingly difficult to retain their place on the land.

Despite the ascendancy of industrialized agriculture, the traditional view of farming as a valuable social and cultural institution has remained alive. Many thoughtful rural people, together with conservationists and naturalists, have maintained that farming should not be thought of simply in economic terms. They have asserted that a harmonious relationship between man and the land is essential to social stability and human welfare. They have protested that any agricultural economy which divorces the vast majority of people from the land, replacing them with machines and technology, is a false economy.

The history of American agriculture has been pronounced a great success story by proponents of industrial agriculture. But in the eyes of many Americans, who are concerned with human beings as well as economics, with a healthy environment as well as efficiency, the course that the nation's agriculture has followed appears tragically mistaken.

This book is composed of the work of more than eighty photographers and encompasses a time span of over a century. Some of these photographers are well-known for their documentation of rural America. Others are obscure. Each has contributed in some way to our image and understanding of life on the land.

However, there are certain photographers whose work stands out as especially important and who call for particular mention. These are the photographers whose images form the heart of the book.

Emma Coleman, whose photographs appear in the first chapter, "The Yeoman," was a remarkable Massachusetts woman who consciously set out in the 1880s to record a way of life that she knew was dying. As she traveled about the countryside, she aimed her camera at those traditional aspects of New England farm life that already in her day had become quaint and outmoded — the patient, lumbering oxen, the farmer broadcasting his seed by hand in the manner of his ancestors. And she recorded these quiet scenes with an infinite sense of grace and poetry.

Solomon Butcher, whose work is so prominent in the third chapter, "The Farmers' Frontier," came to the West in the early 1880s. A thoughtful and observant man, Butcher was struck by the historical importance of what was occurring around him — the rapid emergence of a new American community, together with the vanishing of the frontier. And he recognized that what was happening in his area of central Nebraska was a microcosm of what was taking place over a large area of the West during the period. With feverish energy Butcher set to work photographing the hundreds of settlers who were streaming into his section of the country. The great majority of these photographs have the same format — the pioneer family posed with some of their livestock in front of their sod house. However, the mood of these images varies greatly. While some of Butcher's pioneer families radiate a sense of satisfaction, of optimism and enthusiasm, there are many others whose faces tell of painful hardships and crushing disappointment. In later years, Butcher would continue to document the growth of his area from a frontier region into a settled community — as the soddies were replaced by comfortable frame houses and barns, and the pioneers' small fields of corn were replaced by large acreages of grain. Three of

Butcher's later photographs appear in chapter four, "Triumph of the Cash System."

Lewis Hine — whose striking work appears in two chapters, "A Bare Hard Living" and "Someone Else's Land" — is best known for his photographs of industrial laborers. However, during the early years of the twentieth century, Hine spent much time outside of urban centers, photographing workers on the land. Hine was committed to documenting and exposing to public view the human exploitation that he saw occurring in American society, and as he explored the nation with his camera, he found that in the country as well as in the factories of the cities, gross exploitation was taking place. In Texas and Oklahoma and Kentucky, he found white sharecropper and tenant families trapped in the cotton or tobacco economy with little hope of ever bettering their condition. On the large commercial vegetable and berry farms of the East Coast and in the sugar beet fields of Colorado, he found rural sweatshops where newly arrived immigrant families worked as seasonal laborers — men, women, and children working in the fields for up to sixteen hours a day. With disarming directness, he presented the harsh realities of these farm laborers' and sharecroppers' lives — the little children hauling heavy loads of berries or long cotton sacks, little children with strained and bitter faces. Hine was the first to portray with great sympathy this darker side of American agriculture.

Of all the photographers represented in this book, none has contributed more than Dorothea Lange. Lange first began photographing rural people during the bleak years of the Great Depression. Traveling across the United States with her husband, the eminent agricultural economist Paul S. Taylor, she grew to understand the underlying causes of the human suffering that she saw, and this understanding gave her photographs a special depth. In the Old South, she photographed sharecroppers scratching out a bare existence in the shadow of the crumbling plantation system. Farther west she photographed the victims of the Dust Bowl and the displacement of cotton tenants by tractors. She followed these refugees from dust and mechanization and depression as they took to the highways, heading westward to the squalid migratory labor camps of California. Some of the photographs that she took during these years appear in "The Plantation," "A Bare Hard Living," and "Someone Else's Land."

Lange's intense interest in the relationship between people and the earth did not cease with the Depression. After the 1930s she returned to the countryside once again, but this time to photograph families who had remained firmly rooted on the land. During the Depression, Lange had portrayed, better than any other photographer, the agony of families losing their hold on the land. With the same intensity of feeling, she would capture in later years the joy and contentment of men, women, and children living in harmony with the earth. Some of these later photographs form a part of the sixth chapter, "Roots in the Earth."

Many other photographers could be mentioned whose work is vital to this book: Andrew Dahl, who made hundreds of exquisite views of Wisconsin farm scenes and landscapes during the 1870s. Margaret Morley, who depicted with such sensitivity the simple, self-sufficient way of life of the hill-country farmers of North Carolina at the turn of the century. George François Mugnier and William Wilson, who created a picture of life in the Cotton Kingdom during the 1880s and 1890s — the former working in the vicinity of New Orleans, the latter around Savannah, Georgia. Kosti Ruohomaa, who loved the land so deeply and who, during the 1940s and 1950s, projected this love in his moody, beautiful photographs of small New England farms. Bruce Davidson, who so forcefully portrayed the plight of contemporary black farmworkers on the East Coast.

Together these many skillful and eloquent photographers have given us a valuable portrait of the complex history of the nation's agriculture. They have unfolded for us the many faces of the American farm.

I. THE YEOMAN

"This is really and truly a *country of farmers*," declared a resident of New York state in the early years of American independence. Another early observer affirmed: "Some few towns excepted, we are all tillers of the earth . . . We are a people of cultivators." [1]

The great majority of farmers in the new nation were men who owned their own land and tilled it themselves or with the help of their sons. Hardworking individuals, these yeomen farmers labored the year round from sunrise to sunset to garner from the earth the necessities of life. Spring, summer, and fall were absorbed in plowing, seeding, harrowing, cultivating, harvesting, haymaking, and other fieldwork. When snow covered the ground, there was time for mending harnesses, making hayforks and other tools, threshing grain, and hauling logs. The life of the farmer's wife was equally rigorous, consumed in an endless round of baking, spinning, weaving, sewing clothes for the family, gardening, and looking after her all too numerous offspring. From morning until evening, the whole family was in motion, each member performing his special tasks — from the boy who herded the livestock or rode the plow horse to the grandfather who sat by the fireside shelling corn or caning a chair. Life was inseparable from labor, and even times of relaxation and merrymaking were usually centered around useful work such as apple-butter making or cornhusking.

Despite this continuous toil, the American farmer knew far more comfort and plenty than the European peasant or laborer. Foreign travelers in the United States seldom failed to note the well-being and prosperity of the nation's large population of landowning farmers. Many travelers commented upon the general equality of condition that they observed throughout much of the American countryside — the remarkable lack of poverty and, at the same time, the lack of anything that by European standards would be called wealth or luxury. Describing the country people of New England, one observer wrote: "They are . . . as a body, industrious and thriving, and possess that middle state of property, which so long, and so often, has been termed golden . . . Few are poor, and few are rich." [2]

Although the photographs that appear in this first chapter were made in the late nineteenth century, they are reminiscent of farm life at an earlier time. In fact, many of the farm people pictured in these photographs continued to live in much the same way as their ancestors had lived a hundred years before. While these images are not actual historical documents of early America, they serve to remind us of that time when we were truly a people of cultivators.

In the years following the Revolution, the American yeoman came to symbolize the democratic aspirations of the new republic. Many advocates of the common man believed that, if the United States were to continue in its democratic course, it was imperative that the nation remain a country composed largely of small, landowning farmers. On this sound basis, it was believed, the nation could continue to develop an egalitarian society in which no class was exploited by any other and in which men lived in harmony both with each other and with nature. Although this democratic, agrarian philosophy was espoused by many men of the time, Thomas Jefferson was its most famous exponent, and it has therefore become most closely identified with his name.

Fundamental to the Jeffersonian philosophy was the assertion that the earth was the inheritance of all mankind. Proponents held that the lands of America should be widely and equitably distributed among the people. Land must not be allowed to be engrossed by the wealthy as it had been in Europe. For such engrossment would lead inevitably to the rise of a class of landless peasants and propertyless factory workers.

The Jeffersonians further asserted that there was an inherent spiritual value in the occupation of farming — that the work of the husbandman was more conducive to health, happiness, and virtue than any other occupation of man. The farmer who went out each day to labor in his fields was in continual contact with God's creation, and this contact imbued him with a natural moral strength.

In Jefferson's view, the worst course America could take would be to follow in Britain's footsteps and strive to become a great manufacturing nation — as northern merchants and capitalists of the period were enthusiastically advocating. In a letter to James Madison, he wrote that he trusted the United States would "remain virtuous . . . as long as agriculture is our principal object . . . When we get piled upon one another in large cities, as in Europe, we shall become corrupt as in Europe, and go to eating one another as they do there." [3]

Jefferson was far from alone in such sentiments. Many other men of the time shared his distrust of commerce and cities and hoped to see the nation remain primarily agricultural. In one of his many essays on political economy, Benjamin Franklin wrote: "There seem to be but three ways for a nation to acquire wealth. The first is by *war* . . . This is *robbery*. The second by *commerce*, which is generally *cheating*. The third by *agriculture*, the only *honest way*, wherein man receives a real increase of the seed thrown into the ground, in a kind of continual miracle, wrought by the hand of God in his favour, as a reward for his innocent life and his virtuous industry." [4]

The yeoman farmer whom Jefferson had known and in whom he had placed so much hope was a remarkably independent and resourceful man. Throughout most regions of the country during the period, access to markets was severely limited and the commercial economy was at a relatively primitive stage. As a result, the average farmer and his family followed a frugal and self-sufficing way of life, producing nearly all of their own needs. The bread on the family table was made with corn — or a mixture of corn and rye — grown on the farm and ground at the local gristmill. The sweetening for the porridge was maple syrup, which the family had collected and processed during the early spring, or perhaps honey from the farmer's hives, while the butter and cheese that the family enjoyed represented long hours of careful labor on the part of the farmer's wife and daughters.

Not only did the farm provide all the food that the family required, it also produced such essential manufactures as candles, soap, tools, furniture, and clothing. The family's sheep, together with their patch of flax, provided the raw materials for the homespun worn by all. Every family kept a flock of geese to pluck for feather beds and pillows. The men and boys of the family were skillful and ingenious whittlers, and many evenings were passed fashioning from wood such diverse items as drinking cups, spoons, ax helves, splint brooms, snaths, combs, and buttons.

In regions close to port towns or to navigable rivers, farmers often produced substantial quantities of surplus products for the market. In eastern Pennsylvania, for example, yeoman farmers grew large amounts of wheat and corn for shipment to the sugar plantations of the West Indies, and in certain areas of southern New England, quantities of fresh and salted meat, cheese, and butter were produced for export.

Although most farmers were not well situated in terms of markets and thus were not motivated to produce large surpluses, every farmer endeavored to produce a certain amount of extra goods. With surplus corn, salt pork, hides, cheese, wool, and other commodities, the farmer would purchase at the country store those few articles which he and his family did not themselves produce — such as salt, coffee, gunpowder, indigo dye, ginger, molasses, and iron and tin utensils. Almost all transactions within the community were made by barter. The neighborhood cobbler who made the farmer's children new shoes for the winter was perhaps paid with a barrel of cider, while the local miller received for his services a portion of the cornmeal which he ground.

By European standards, American agriculture at the beginning of the nineteenth century was crude and backward. The great bulk of American farmers showed little knowledge or interest concerning beneficial crop rotations; their fields were poorly cultivated and their livestock often ill cared for. Worst of all, the majority of farmers made little or no attempt to adequately manure their cropland.

Travelers from abroad often remarked caustically upon these "ignorant," "slovenly," and "wasteful" farming practices. However, the American farmer doubtless felt that his methods were justified by his circumstances. Unlike the European peasant, the American lived in a country of cheap and abundant land. His own farm probably encompassed from 100 to 400 acres, of which he used only a small portion as cropland. Under these conditions, there seemed little reason to adopt more intensive agricultural methods. While his fields might show a lack of care and attention, his farm still yielded his family all the food and fiber that they could use and provided them with a comfortable subsistence.

Neighborly cooperation was an important ingredient in early American farm life — as it would continue to be in later years. "Good neighborship," as one contemporary termed it, was expressed in a great variety of ways, from helping out in times of illness to the practice of "changing works." In many communities it was customary for a farmer who was slaughtering a large animal to parcel out sections to various neighbors and, in this way, families provided each other with fresh meat on a fairly regular basis. "Bees" and "frolics" were gotten up for a great variety of purposes, making it possible to accomplish large, time-consuming tasks such as cornhusking and field clearing with relative speed, and often turning dull, tedious, or arduous work into occasions for lively sociability.

In the custom of house-raising and barn-raising, the spirit of cooperation and mutual aid among American farmers reached dramatic heights. On such occasions, a dozen or more farmers would come together to help out a neighbor. A full day would be spent in strenuous and backbreaking labor, the workers expecting to receive no more immediate reward than a hearty dinner and the good cheer of pleasant company. The life of the average farm family in early America may have been arduous and spare, yet it appears to have lacked nothing in good fellowship and neighborliness.

 "The great business of the continent is agriculture," wrote Benjamin Franklin in 1784. "For one artisan or merchant, I suppose, we have at least one hundred farmers, by far the greatest part cultivators of their own fertile lands, from whence many of them draw, not only the food necessary for their subsistence, but materials of their clothing . . .

"Whoever . . . views here the happy mediocrity that so generally prevails throughout these States, where the cultivator works for himself, and supports his family in decent plenty, will, methinks, see abundant reason to bless Divine Providence . . . and be convinced that no nation known to us enjoys a greater share of human felicity."

Spring plowing. New England, 1899. GEORGE TINGLEY

Elm tree. Massachusetts, c. 1880. EMMA COLEMAN

Oxcart. Maine, 1884. EMMA COLEMAN

Sowing grain. Maine, 1885.
EMMA COLEMAN

Massachusetts, c. 1880. EMMA COLEMAN

"There were no landlords in this country," wrote the son of a New England farmer, describing farm life in the 1820s and '30s. "Almost every man owned the land he cultivated . . . The proprietor of hundreds of acres worked harder than any man he could hire . . .

"No one ever spoke of incomes; they were not much reckoned. The farmer who made both ends meet, with a little increase of his stock, thought himself doing well enough . . .

"In winter . . . the farmers harnessed up their teams, loaded their large double sleighs with their surplus produce — hogs frozen stiff and packed down in snow, tallow, butter, cheese, dried apples, apple sauce, honey, home-made cloth, woolen socks and mittens — and, with the jingle of merry bells, drove off one or two hundred miles to Boston to sell their loads, and bring home salt, sugar, molasses, rum . . . and other foreign luxuries."

Digging potatoes. Maine, c. 1880. EMMA COLEMAN

Child driving cow. Maine, 1883. EMMA COLEMAN

Gristmill. North Carolina, c. 1900. MARGARET MORLEY

Clearing land with oxen. North Carolina, c. 1900. MARGARET MORLEY

"The class of citizens who provide at once their own food and raiment, may be viewed as the most truly independent," wrote James Madison in 1792. "It follows, that the greater the proportion of this class to the whole society, the more free, the more independent, and the more happy must be the society itself."

Spinning wool. North Carolina, c. 1900. MARGARET MORLEY

Apple-paring bee. North Carolina, c. 1900. MARGARET MORLEY

Fields with shocks of corn. North Carolina, c. 1900. Photographer unknown.

Gathering apples. Maine, c. 1880. EMMA COLEMAN

Passing through New England in the early 1800s, one traveler observed, "The generality of people live in easy independent circumstances; and upon that footing of equality which is best calculated to promote virtue and happiness among society."

Shelling corn. New England, c. 1900. CHANSONETTA EMMONS

Wisconsin, c. 1875. ANDREW DAHL

Wisconsin, c. 1875. ANDREW DAHL

In the first years of American independence, Thomas Jefferson wrote:

"The earth is given as a common stock for man to labor and live on . . . It is not too soon to provide by every possible means that as few as possible shall be without a little portion of land. The small land holders are the most precious part of a state."

Haying.
Wisconsin, c. 1875.
ANDREW DAHL

II. THE PLANTATION

We [in the South] have gentlemen and gentlewomen . . ." boasted a wealthy cotton planter in 1861. "We have a system which enables us to reap the fruits of the earth by a race which we save from barbarism . . . whilst we are enabled to cultivate the arts, the graces and accomplishments of life . . . and to understand the affairs of the country." [1]

The "system" of which this planter boasted had been evolving and expanding in the South for 200 years. During the Colonial period, slavery and the plantation system had developed around the production of tobacco in the coastal regions of Virginia and Maryland and around the production of rice and indigo in South Carolina and Georgia. By the time of the Revolution, vast plantations had arisen in these regions and slaves had come to constitute one half of the population of Virginia and two thirds of the population of South Carolina.

However, the great expansion of slavery and the plantation across the entire South came with the introduction of cotton as a staple crop. Shortly after the Revolution, England's demand for cotton fiber underwent a sudden increase due to innovations in the manufacture of textiles and the growth of cotton mills. During this period, cotton production in the United States had been limited by the difficulty of separating the seed from the lint. However, the invention of the cotton gin by Eli Whitney in 1793 solved this problem and permitted cotton to be grown on a large scale.

The introduction of Whitney's gin was followed by a prodigious expansion of cotton production in the South. In the early 1800s, cotton swept over the uplands of South Carolina and Georgia, transforming an area of small diversified farms into one dominated by slave plantations. In succeeding years cotton planters would move westward into one region after another — the largest slaveholders always monopolizing the most fertile tracts of land and leaving behind the less desirable areas for the smaller farmers. In the 1820s and 1830s, planters and their troops of slaves streamed into the lower Mississippi valley region and into the Black Belt of Alabama. Two decades later, planters were buying up lands in the Black Prairie of Texas and the alluvial lands of Arkansas.

Cotton production during these years soared. In the thirty years following Whitney's invention, cotton output jumped from 16,000 bales to 450,000, and by the time of the Civil War, it had climbed to 4,500,000 bales. "Cotton is King," the South proclaimed, and indeed it seemed so, for the value of this single crop exceeded the combined value of all other United States exports.

The great profits to be reaped from cotton growing created a booming market for slaves. Since importation of Africans had been legally blocked at the beginning of the century, a brisk interstate trade developed, with dealers buying up surplus slaves in the upper South and selling them to planters in the southwest. In the three decades preceding the Civil War, at least 150,000 slaves from Virginia alone were sold to dealers, and travelers in the South frequently noted in their journals having encountered coffles of blacks being driven to the new cotton regions. Increasing demand for slaves caused prices to sky-rocket. Whereas at the time of the Revolution a "prime field hand" was selling for $200, by 1860 planters were paying $1800.

In the 1830s, a visitor in the area of Natchez, Mississippi, reported on the mood of excitement and speculation that had enveloped planters in the region. He wrote: "Cotton and ne-groes are the constant theme — the ever harped upon, never worn out subject of conversation . . . To sell cotton in order to buy negroes — to make more cotton to buy more negroes, 'ad infinitum,' is the aim and tendency of all the operations of the thorough-going cotton planter; his whole soul is wrapped up in the pursuit. It is, apparently, the principle by which he 'lives, moves, and has his being.' " [2]

The spread of slavery across the South caused Southerners to reevaluate their attitude toward their "peculiar institution." During the Revolutionary period, the humanitarian principles of the Declaration of Independence had made a deep impression upon Southerners as well as Northerners. Many leading south-ern spokesmen of the time had concluded that human bondage was incompatible with the doctrine of natural rights and the ideals of the Revolution. Thomas Jefferson had drawn up plans for the gradual emancipation of Virginia's slave population, and liberal Southerners, in general, were hopeful that the institution which they had inherited from their fathers would with time pass into oblivion. This lack of enthusiasm for slavery was strengthened by the current economic condition of the upper South, where the steady decline in tobacco prices was making slavery far less profitable than it had formerly been.

However, farther down the coast the great rice plantations of South Carolina continued to flourish. And the rapid rise of cot-ton as a staple crop gave new life to the plantation system and dampened antislavery sentiment throughout the South. While planters in the cotton country — and also in the booming sugar region around New Orleans — were eagerly purchasing field hands, the old tobacco region of the upper South was finding a new and important source of income in the flourishing traffic in slaves. As the Cotton Kingdom extended its domain and in-creasing wealth was invested in human chattels, the thought of eventual abolition became ever more remote. The wealth and power of the southern oligarchy had come to depend upon slavery, and the perpetuation of the institution became imper-ative.

Soon southern statesmen were propounding a social philosophy that upheld slavery as a "positive good" and boldly rejected the doctrine of natural rights. "I repudiate, as ridiculously absurd," wrote one South Carolina governor, the "dogma of Mr. Jefferson, that 'all men are born equal.' " [3] Instead, it was argued that the natural proclivity of mankind was to divide itself into dominant and subservient classes, and that the highest form of civilization could only be attained when society was permitted to develop this natural stratification. "I hold it [slavery] to be a good," declared John C. Calhoun. "Moreover, there never has yet existed a wealthy and civilized society in which one portion of the community did not in point of fact live on the labor of the other." [4] The president of a Virginia college wrote: "It is as much in the order of nature that men should enslave each other as that other animals should prey upon each other." [5]

During the three decades preceding the Civil War, the virtues of slavery were loudly proclaimed by politicians, the press, and the pulpit all across the South. Not only was the institution defended as ethically sound, it was further asserted that the slave himself greatly benefited from his servitude. In return for his industry and obedience, the slave received from his master the assurance that he would be cared for for the duration of his life, and thus he was relieved of the insecurity and anxiety which hounded the free laborer. "Our slaves," declared one cotton planter, "are the happiest . . . human beings on whom the sun shines." [6]

The work day on a cotton plantation began before dawn. "Every morning at four o'clock the overseer blowed a conchshell," recalled one former slave, "and all us Niggers knowed it was time to get up and go to work . . . Everybody worked from sunup 'till sundown. If we didn't get up when we was supposed to we got a beating." [7]

Cotton, like the other plantation staples — tobacco, rice, and sugar — was a demanding crop, requiring attention throughout almost three fourths of the year. From dawn to darkness, gangs of male and female slaves labored under the direction and constant prodding of their master or an overseer or a black "driver." In winter and early spring, the fields were plowed and seeded. In late spring the cotton was "chopped" and cultivated in order to kill weeds. Then from September to December came the long picking season. When slaves were not occupied with cotton, they were employed in planting and cultivating corn, "pulling fodder," perhaps raising another food crop such as sweet potatoes, clearing new land, digging and clearing ditches, and numerous other tasks.

It was economically imperative for the planter to exact as much labor from his slaves as possible. And his managerial skills were directed at seeing that his work force was always productive and never idle. On the other hand, the increasing market value of slaves made it decidedly uneconomic for him to press his bondsmen to the point of complete exhaustion and physical breakdown. As one southern agricultural journal observed in 1849: "The time has been that the farmer could kill up and wear out one Negro to buy another; but it is not so now. Negroes are too high in proportion to the price of cotton, and it behooves those who own them to make them last as long as possible." [8]

Many planters took considerable interest in maintaining the health of their "people" — instructing their overseers not to "over-drive" field hands and specifying that a rest period be allowed during the hottest part of the day. Planters were also interested in perpetuating and increasing their labor force, and "breeding women" and "sucklers" — as pregnant or nursing women were called — were usually assigned less strenuous workloads than other slaves.

However, in the race for wealth, there were always many planters who ignored their long-term interests and drove their laborers beyond the point of human endurance. Often such planters hired overseers who publicly boasted of being hard drivers and of bringing in big crops each harvest no matter what the human cost. One old woman, recalling her years as a slave, related:

"I never knowed what it was to rest. I just work all de time from mornin' till late at night. I had to do everythin' dey was to do on de outside. Work in de field, chop wood, hoe corn, till sometime I feels like my back surely break . . . Lordy, I'se took a thousand lashins in my day . . . Dey didn't care how old or how young you were, you never too big to get de lash." [9]

The expansion of cotton across the South entailed not only incalculable human exploitation, but also exploitation of the land. In pursuit of quick fortunes, enormous acreages were planted continuously to cotton, with no thought being given to maintaining the fertility of the soil. When the lands were worn out and ceased to yield remunerative crops, the planter with his family and troop of slaves would remove to the west, buy new land, and settle down once more to growing as much cotton as physically possible.

On most cotton plantations the only other crop planted extensively was corn, which, together with fat salt pork, constituted the basic rations of the slave population. But many planters, in their single-minded devotion to cotton, failed even to raise sufficient provisions to feed their own slaves and were obliged to purchase much corn and pork from the North.

For large numbers of planters, the only concern was how much cotton there was to sell at the end of the year. There were very few who cared that they were also selling the fertility of the land. Shortly before the Civil War, the editor of a southern agricultural paper wrote: "The system is such that the planter scarcely considers his land as part of his permanent investment. It is rather a part of his current expenses . . . He buys land, uses it until it is exhausted and then sells it . . . for whatever it will bring. It is with him a perishable or movable property. It is something to be worn out, not improved." [10]

In the War Between the States, the planter class lost its great wealth in slaves, and many proud estates were reduced to rubble. Yet the plantation system itself was not destroyed.

After the war, the federal government failed to grant to the newly freed blacks their longed-for "forty acres and a mule," and the great estates were not confiscated, as many planters had feared. Instead, the basic elements of the plantation economy remained largely intact. While slavery had been abolished, there nevertheless remained in the South a mass of propertyless and dependent black laborers. The market demand for cotton continued strong, and there were landlords and capitalists who were willing to finance the growing of the crop.

After a period of experimentation in which the freedmen were employed as wage laborers, the plantation system was firmly reestablished on the basis of sharecropping. Under this arrangement, the landlord assigned his sharecroppers plots of from fifteen to twenty-five acres and provided them with work stock, equipment, and seed, together with a cabin. When the crops were harvested, one-half went to the cropper as payment for his labor. The landlord further agreed to "furnish" his sharecroppers, i.e., to provide them on credit with the food and other supplies which they needed to get through the long growing season. Since the cost of such advances was always high, at "settling time" most of the sharecropper's slender earnings were absorbed in paying off his debts. The black man was no longer legally a slave, yet poverty and ignorance, white intimidation and extortion effectively kept many sharecroppers in a position of helpless bondage.

The perpetuation of the plantation system meant the perpetuation of many of the South's most serious problems. In the years following the Civil War, the region's self-destructive obsession with cotton would grow even more intense, and self-sufficiency in the production of foodstuffs would decline. Vast tracts of once-fertile soil would continue to be reduced to barren and gullied wastes, while rural poverty in the South remained more pronounced than in any other area of the nation.

In shame and frustration, many white Southerners blamed

their region's agricultural failure on their black labor force — the very labor force that they themselves had created and that they were unwilling to live without. This pathetic irony is strikingly set forth in the public address of a Georgia governor near the turn of the century:

"We have not diversified our crops because the Negro has not been willing to diversify . . . We have not improved our soil because the Negro is not willing to . . . leave his cotton seed to be returned to the fields that he has denuded of humus and all possible traces of fertility. Because he is unwilling to handle heavy plows we have permitted him to scratch the land with his scooter just deep enough for all the soil to be washed from the surface, leaving our fields practically barren and wasted. We have not raised stock on the farm because the Negro is cruelly inhuman and starves the work animals . . . We have accepted his thriftless and destructive methods simply because we have not been able to do without him." [11]

On the eve of the Civil War, a leading South Carolina statesman and planter declared:

"In all social systems there must be a class to do the mean duties, to perform the drudgery of life . . . Such a class you must have, or you would not have that other class which leads progress, refinement, and civilization. It constitutes the very mud-sills of society and of political government; and you might as well attempt to build a house in the air, as to build either the one or the other, except on the mud-sills. Fortunately for the South, she found a race adapted to that purpose to her hand. A race inferior to herself, but eminently qualified in temper, in vigor, in docility, in capacity to stand the climate, to answer all her purposes. We use them for the purpose, and call them slaves . . .

"The greatest strength of the South arises from the harmony of her political and social institutions. This harmony gives her a frame of society, the best in the world, and an extent of political freedom . . . such as no other people ever enjoyed upon the face of the earth . . . The South is satisfied, content, happy, harmonious, and prosperous."

Slave family, South Carolina cotton plantation, 1862. T. H. O'SULLIVAN

Driver and gang, returning from cotton fields. South Carolina, c. 1860. G. N. BARNARD

"Niggers and cotton; cotton and niggers; these are the law and the prophets to the men of the South," asserted a traveler in the 1850s.

Another traveler wrote: "A plantation well-stocked with hands is . . . every man's ambition who resides at the south . . . Not till Mississippi becomes one vast cotton field, will this mania, which has entered into the very marrow, bone and sinew of a Mississippian's system, pass away. And not then, till the lands become exhausted and wholly unfit for further cultivation."

Pickers and overseer. Place, date, and photographer unknown.

43

Slave quarters on a Georgia cotton plantation, c. 1880. WILLIAM WILSON

"Marse Lewis had a heap of slaves," recalled a former Georgia slave. "The overseer, he had a bugle what he blowed to wake up the slaves. He blowed it long before day so that they could eat breakfast and be out there in the fields waiting for the sun to rise so they could see how to work, and they stayed out there and worked 'till black dark.

"When a rainy spell come and the grass got to growing fast, they worked them slaves at night, even when the moon warn't shining. On them dark nights one set of slaves held lanterns for the others to see how to chop the weeds out of the cotton and corn. Work was sure tight in them days. Every slave had a task to do after they got back to them cabins at night."

Slave family. Georgia, c. 1860. HAVENS

Planting sweet potatoes on a South Carolina cotton plantation, 1862. Attributed to H. P. MOORE

Magnolia Plantation, Louisiana, c. 1890.
Photographer unknown.

Cotton bales, New Orleans waterfront, c. 1885. GEORGE FRANÇOIS MUGNIER

"It may be doubted whether any river in the world can exhibit so magnificent a spectacle as the Mississippi," wrote a visitor to New Orleans in the 1840s. "A greater number of large, handsome, and fine vessels seemed to me to line the magnificent curve of the Mississippi, than I had ever seen in any one port . . .

"The Levee itself, on the edge of which all these ships and vessels are anchored, is covered with bales of cotton and other merchandise; and in the busy season . . . is filled with buyers and sellers, from every part of the Union, and spectators from every part of the world . . .

"Such incessant bustle, that every body and every thing seems to be in perpetual motion."

New Orleans waterfront, c. 1885. GEORGE FRANÇOIS MUGNIER

Worker at the Cotton Exchange, Savannah, c. 1880. WILLIAM WILSON

*Steamer leaving Baton Roug
with 3000 bales of cotton, 189
A. D. LYT*

Sharecropper cabins on a Mississippi cotton plantation, 1940. MARION POST WOLCOTT

"[After the War] the colored folks stayed with the old boss man and farmed and worked on the plantations," related a former Alabama sharecropper. "The boss man built them homes and let them live there. They were still slaves, but they were free slaves — they could go anywhere they pleased. They were unfree slaves before the Civil War and free slaves after.

"When I was coming up, they got to where they would build your houses and give you something to eat. Once a year you'd get clothes or cloth. You'd go every Friday night to get your ration. When you got your own crop and were paid for it, why then you'd pay your ration back. You raised your own cotton, but if the boss man fed you — which he did — then he got the cotton. I would say it was just a few days ago where the wind blowed where you could tell the difference."

North Carolina, c. 1930. DORIS ULMANN

53

Sharecropper cultivating cotton. Georgia, 1937. DOROTHEA LANGE

"The Negro skins the land and the landlord skins the Negro," declared one southern governor.

Sharecropper family chopping cotton. Alabama, 1937. DOROTHEA LANGE

Sharecropper. Mississippi, 1937. DOROTHEA LANGE

Alabama, 1938. DOROTHEA LANGE

Georgia, 1941.
JACK DELANO

"Cotton is master of them all," reflected a southern writer. "All men in the South are slaves of cotton, prospering as those white fields flourish, and failing as they fail."

Erosion. Georgia, 1941. JACK DELANO

III. THE FARMERS' FRONTIER

Throughout the nation's history, American farmers had been on the move, their hopes and ambitions turned toward the West. In the three decades following 1870, this westward stream of migration swelled into a flood, spilling over the remainder of the Prairies, over the Plains and the Pacific Coast, and sweeping away the farmer's last frontier. During this brief span of time more land was taken up than in all the previous history of the country.

The rapid settlement of the last frontier was stimulated, in part, by the availability of free land under the Homestead Act. It was further stimulated by the construction of transcontinental railroad lines and a multitude of branch lines. Railroads not only expedited passage to the frontier and opened up new areas for settlement, they also launched a vigorous colonization campaign, inundating the East and Europe with extravagant promotional literature portraying the unknown territories as a virtual garden of Eden.

Many families who came west in the last decades of the century would succeed in building comfortable and fruitful lives in the new country. But many others — particularly those who came after 1880 — would find that the West failed to live up to their expectations. Some families with little capital who came in search of free land would discover that most of the good land was already in the hands of railroads or speculators and that only inferior tracts were left open to the homesteader. Some, who moved out optimistically onto the semiarid Plains, would see their crops, together with their dreams, wither and die under the unrelenting sun as they waited helplessly for the rains that never came.

Western expansion in the United States had always been accompanied by an intense and, at times, frenzied spirit of speculation. Millions of acres of fertile virgin soil waiting to be claimed — "oceans of land . . . good as the best in America, and yet lying without occupants." [1] The thought of such bounty was enough to stir the ambitions of most men. The great frontier was a temptation to men, both rich and poor, to try their luck at turning a quick profit. The eastern capitalist could purchase a township of raw prairie land, hoping that a boom in the area would soon double or treble the value of his investment. The farmer of moderate means was tempted to buy an extra quarter section in the expectation of selling it in a few years to some newcomer at a handsome profit.

The lure of the frontier tugged at farmers in the older states and awakened a mood of restlessness. When neighbors here and there sold out to take up land farther west, many farmers found the urge to follow irresistible. Large numbers of those who struck out for the frontier were landless men with little opportunity at home — the younger sons of small farmers, renters, and farmhands unable to afford eastern farms, or European immigrants. But there were also settlers on the frontier who had left behind comparatively productive farms in order to seek their fortunes in the new country. For many families, mobility became an accepted part of life, some moving westward three or four times within a generation. Although the process of uprooting was always painful, the chance of improving the family's economic position took precedence over old friendships and family and community ties. In the 1850s, one observer of the American scene remarked:

"It has appeared to me that there is less attachment among our countrymen to their birth place, or the family homestead, than almost any civilized people on earth . . . the roving propensity of the Yankee is proverbial. Our actions but too clearly indicate us as mere 'pilgrims and sojourners on earth,' ready to settle down in one place, and then break up and re-settle in another, just as interest shall seem most likely, in our estimation, to be promoted." [2]

The widespread speculation in public land which characterized the nation's frontier period had never been either restricted or restrained by government land policy. On the contrary, the government had generally accepted the idea that a substantial part of the public lands would be purchased by men of wealth purely for investment purposes. As a result, a large portion of the public domain was acquired by capitalists, real-estate companies, banks, and other large purchasers.

This engrossment of public lands by wealthy speculators was deeply resented by most settlers on the frontier. During the 1840s and 1850s, these Westerners and their political allies brought ever-increasing pressure to bear on Congress to call a halt to the rampant monopolization of the public domain and to make government land policy more favorable to settlers of little means. Westerners demanded that "the public lands . . . be held as a sacred reserve for the cultivator of the soil," and it was further demanded that small tracts of government land be granted free to actual settlers. [3]

In 1862, western settlers won an historic victory when, after years of political wrangling, the Homestead Act was finally passed. Under this act, Congress granted 160 acres free to any settler who would undertake to improve his claim and live on it for a period of five years. The Homestead Act did not guarantee that the remainder of the public domain would be reserved for actual settlers only, as reformers had wished. Nevertheless, it was widely hoped that the passage of this liberal legislation signaled a decisive change in the direction of government land policy and that in the future the activity of large-scale speculators would be sharply curtailed.

The optimism surrounding the passage of the Homestead Act would soon prove to be ill-founded. In the years that followed, Congress continued to permit enormous tracts of public land to be engrossed by wealthy investors and speculators. Much of the best agricultural land in the country was not reserved for homesteading, but instead left open to sale, and investors continued to purchase vast holdings directly from the government. At the same time, other speculators were being allowed to amass hundreds of thousands of acres through the lax and often corrupt administration of various land laws — such as the Desert Land Act, the Preemption Act, and even the Homestead Act. Although Congress had adopted a policy of granting free homesteads to frontier settlers, the westward movement remained, as it had been in the past, a wild scramble for land in which the most powerful interests won the largest prize.

In the race for land, the nation's railroads were by far the largest single winners. During the years immediately following the passage of the Homestead Act, railroads succeeded in wresting from Congress increasingly larger grants of public land. In 1862, the two lines that built the first transcontinental railroad received, along the length of their right of way, ten square miles of land for each mile of track constructed. Two years later, another transcontinental line was granted up to forty square miles for each mile of track. It has been estimated that the total amount of public land bestowed on railroad corporations during the second part of the nineteenth century by both federal and state governments amounted to approximately 180 million acres — an area almost one-tenth the size of the United States.

The government's lavish grants to railroads together with the prodigious activity of real-estate investors substantially reduced the amount of public land that was open to homesteading. Many settlers who came west to find free land discovered that fertile, well-located land open to homesteading was more difficult to come by than they had expected. Railroad lines, which usually preceded settlers into new territories, had picked out, as part of their grants, much of the best agricultural land throughout large regions of the West and were advertising it for sale. Speculators and land companies, which had also moved in early, had swallowed up other large sections of desirable land. Many settlers and their families found that in order to locate free land it was necessary to move into unsettled and isolated areas, miles away from transportation lines, schools, churches, and other community institutions. Moreover, in many cases, the government land available was agriculturally inferior to the lands held by railroads and speculators.

In view of this situation, it is not surprising that many settlers decided to buy their farms rather than to homestead. Of the 2.5 million farms that were established in the public-land states between 1860 and 1900, it has been estimated that only one in five were legally acquired homesteads.

As free land grew scarcer in the more humid areas of the Plains during the late 1870s, frontier farmers began to push farther westward — moving out beyond the 100th meridian into western Kansas, Nebraska, and eastern Colorado. During this period, the agricultural potential of this semiarid region had been the subject of much heated debate between government scientists and western interests. Scientists for the U.S. Geological Survey, together with army officers who had explored the Plains, in general maintained that most of the region was incapable of sustaining crop farming. It was argued that the semiarid lands should be reserved for grazing purposes or for irrigated farming. And it was deemed imperative that prospective settlers be warned of the dangers inherent in moving out into the dry country.

However, both in Congress and in the West, the voices of these government scientists were drowned out by the far louder and more numerous voices of western promoters. Railroad companies pictured the Plains as an agricultural paradise where settlers would "all become prosperous, and many will acquire fortunes in a short period." One railroad, selling lands in western Kansas and eastern Colorado, declared that "Crops of all kinds . . . can be raised in abundance without much labor, and our fruits are unsurpassed in size and delicacy of flavor." [4] Western boosters claimed that rainfall on the Plains was steadily increasing from year to year, and much publicity was given to the theory that "rain follows the plow." Proponents of this popular theory asserted that as farmers moved westward planting crops and trees, the climate of the region would inevitably grow more humid.

Plentiful rainfall on the Plains during the mid-1880s seemed to justify this widespread optimism. And eager land-seekers rushed westward to stake their claims. Land offices in Kansas, Nebraska, and Colorado were deluged with applications for government land. In 1886, land entries in Kansas amounted to over 5 million acres — about one tenth of the entire area of the state — and virtually all of this acreage lay beyond the 100th meridian. At the land office in Garden City, Kansas, on the 101st meridian, 50,000 acres were taken daily during the year 1885. The register of this land office wrote:

"The rush for land in this section of Kansas is unprecedented. Every train brings in a crowd of landseekers. For more than an hour before the office opens, a mass of humanity throngs the doorway, and it is a remarkable sight to see the press and excitement." [5]

The great land boom on the Central Plains frontier proved to be short-lived. In the late 1880s a series of dry years began in the region which would continue through the middle of the next decade. Years of partial or total crop failure inflicted terrible suffering on new settlers on this frontier and caused many to abandon their claims. Between 1888 and 1892, half of the population of western Kansas moved out and large areas in Nebraska and Colorado were almost entirely depopulated. From the drought-stricken regions came reports of "hundreds of families . . . on the verge of starvation . . ." and urgent pleas for food, fuel, and seed for the next year's crop.[6] One Kansas settler wrote:

"Most all the people here that could leave have done so and what is here are too poor they cannot get away and are in need for they been here for four years and raised no crops."[7]

By 1890, nearly all of the most desirable agricultural land in the country had passed into private hands. On the Pacific Coast only forested uplands and land requiring costly irrigation remained to be settled. In the Dakotas and Texas, settlement was pushing up against the 100th meridian, and in the Central Plains, farmers had already far exceeded the line of safety.

Yet there was one large region of well-watered and highly desirable land in the nation that had only just begun to be settled — the region that would soon become known as Oklahoma Territory. During the 1820s this territory had been set aside as a perpetual Indian reserve — "a permanent home . . ." according to one treaty, "which shall, under the most solemn guarantee of the United States, be and remain theirs forever . . ."[8] This solemn pledge would not endure long. Throughout the 1880s land-hungry white settlers had clamored for the federal government to open up the territory for homesteading. On several occasions, groups of "boomers," as they were called, moved illegally into Indian lands and had to be forcefully ejected by federal troops.

In the end, however, the government gave in to the insistent demands of the land-seekers, and the Indians, as usual, were pushed aside. In the spring of 1889, it was announced that 2 million acres in the central region of the territory would be opened to homesteading. Days prior to the official opening, thousands of prospective settlers converged on the borders of the former Indian lands, where they set up camps and waited restlessly, held in check by federal troops.

At precisely twelve noon on the appointed day soldiers fired their pistols, signaling the opening, and the furious race for land began. One reporter at the scene wrote:

"Along the line as far as the eye could reach, with a shout and a yell the swift riders shot out, then followed the light buggies or wagons and last the lumbering prairie schooners and freighters' wagons . . . — above all a great cloud of dust hovering like smoke over a battlefield. It was a wild scramble, a rough and tumble contest filled with excitement and real peril." [9]

By the end of the day, hundreds of settlers had staked out farms, and two tent cities with 10,000 residents each had sprung up on the prairie.

The "land run" of 1889 was only the beginning of white incursions into former Oklahoma Indian lands. In succeeding years, other portions of Indian territory would be opened for settlement and more runs would be held. By far the largest, most famous, and most violent of these stampedes took place in the Cherokee Outlet, which was opened in 1893. In this spectacular run some 100,000 land-seekers competed against each other to obtain one of 40,000 claims. In the melee, several people lost their lives, and as night came on, men sat guarding their claims with rifles.

Like pioneers on other frontiers, the land-seekers who swarmed into Oklahoma came with a variety of motives and intentions. Some were petty speculators who came merely to stake a claim and sell out at the first opportunity. Most were poor men — renters and small farmers — who yearned for the chance to begin life anew on the rich prairie soil of which they had heard such glowing accounts. The wife of one Oklahoma settler who moved to the territory in 1890 wrote:

"We were going to God's Country. Eighteen hundred and 90 . . . It was pretty hard to part with some of our things. We didn't have much but we had worked hard for everything we had. You had to work hard in that rocky country in Missouri. I was glad to be leaving it . . . We were going to God's Country. We were going to a new land and get rich. Then we could have a real home of our own." [10]

During the last three decades of the nineteenth century, a vast migration of settlers streamed into the new states and territories of the West. They came in high hopes, lured on by the promise of free homesteads, by flamboyant advertisements for cheap railroad land, and by their own keen ambitions.

In the 1870s, a young man homesteading in Nebraska wrote home to Indiana: "Ma you can see just as far as you please here and almost every foot in sight can be plowed . . . A man can come here with $500 and manage properly and in a few years he can have a good comfortable home in a beautiful looking country . . .

An ex-tenant farmer, now homesteading in Kansas, wrote back to friends in Illinois: "My advice is to quit paying high rents, come to Sumner County, Kansas, preempt a quarter section of land, improve and enter it, and make a home where you can enjoy all the comforts of life; where you will feel independent, and by energy will soon gain a fortune."

Homestead. Nebraska, 188
SOLOMON BUTCH

Nebraska, c. 1886. SOLOMON BUTCHER

Nebraska, c. 1886. SOLOMON BUTCHER

"Here is a place for a man to rebuild his fortune again,"
declared the Dakota territorial legislature. "Here there need be
no destitute, for all that will work there is abundance; here is a
land yielding bountifully, open to all nations, where all may
enjoy the blessings of a home."

"HO! FOR THE WEST!" proclaimed a railroad broadside.
"Nebraska ahead! The truth will out! The best farming and
stock raising country in the world! The great central region, not
too hot nor too cold . . .

"The population now pouring into this region consists of
shrewd and well-informed farmers who *know* what is good, and
are taking advantage of the opportunities offered.

"The crops . . . are as fine as can be: a large wheat and barley
crop has been harvested; corn is in splendid condition and all
other crops are equally fine. The opportunities now offered to
buy B. & M. R.R. lands on long credit, low interest . . . will never
again be found.

"Go and see for yourself."

Russian immigrants. South Dakota, 1894. Photographer unknown.

As the public domain rapidly diminished, poor men and rich men alike rushed frantically to snap up the remaining lands.

In 1880, one Kansas resident wrote: "The area of cheap and agricultural lands is growing to a small circumference. But a few years more and such lands will be owned and occupied, and the present generation will see them rise in value until they will pass beyond the reach of the poor man . . . Never before in the history of the country has there been so many of our people looking with longing eyes toward the few remaining sections that yet remain to invite them to possess and occupy."

In 1885, the Commissioner of the General Land Office reported: "The near approach of the period when the United States will have no land to dispose of has stimulated the exertions of capitalists and corporations to acquire outlying regions of public land in mass by whatever means, legal or illegal, while the imminent exhaustion of lands in the more thickly settled states has aroused an excitement in the land districts in such states to a degree that pursuit of lands has become a headlong race."

U.S. Land Office, Garden City, Kansas, 1885. Fifty-thousand acres taken daily. Photographer unknown.

Oregon Trail. Wyoming, c. 1875. W. H. JACKSON

Colorado, c. 1885. Photographer unknown.

In the search for good farmland with plenty of rainfall, many settlers crossed the arid Plains to homestead on the Pacific Coast. By the 1890s, the best agricultural lands in Oregon and Washington had been claimed, and newcomers to these states turned to the heavily wooded regions where they set to work hacking out "stump farms."

In California, almost all of the desirable farmland had been taken up decades earlier — much of it in large tracts by speculators and men of wealth. In 1870, one California farmer wrote:

"There is plenty of land for sale in California, but at prices ranging far beyond the means of the ordinary immigrant . . . The fact is well known, that the majority of the available lands are held by speculators, at prices far beyond the reach of a poor man."

Stump farm. Washington, 1900
DARIUS KINSE

Clearing a homestead. Washington, c. 1900. FRITZ SETHE

Stump farm. Washington, 1906. C. H. PARK

"Oklahoma — The Last Chance!" proclaimed a handbill announcing the opening of a fertile tract of former Indian lands to white settlement.

The first Oklahoma "land run" was held in 1889. It was followed by others in 1891, '92, and '93. In these desperate stampedes, thousands of land-hungry settlers raced to stake claims on the former Oklahoma Indian lands.

Wagons moving into Oklahoma Indian lands for the land run of 1889. W. S. PRETTYMAN

Prospective Oklahoma settlers waiting for the land run of 1889. Photographer unknown.

Wagons lined up just before the start of the Oklahoma land run of 1893. W. S. PRETTYMAN

Oklahoma land run in the Cherokee Outlet, 1893. W. S. PRETTYMAN

Homestead claim. Oklahoma Territory, 1889. A. P. SWEARINGEN

"We are having a bad time generally in our county this fall," wrote a Kansas farmer in the 1880s. "Have not had rain enough since the 10th of July to wet the ground two inches deep. Wheat and rye that was sown two months ago are dead. Some of it came up and some just sprouted in the ground, but it is all dead."

In the pursuit of free land, many home-seekers pushed far out into the semiarid regions of the Great Plains. In years of adequate rainfall, these homesteaders might, for a time, prosper. Yet when the dry times inevitably returned, settlers faced ruin. After a period of severe drought beginning in the late 1880s and continuing into the next decade, hundreds of thousands of settlers retreated from western Kansas and Nebraska. In a plea for help, the wife of one Kansas homesteader wrote:

"I take my pen in hand to let you know that we are starving to death. It is pretty hard to do without anything to eat in this God-forsaken country . . . If I was in Iowa I would be all right. I was born there and raised there."

Abandoned homestead
Western Kansas, 1897
W. D. JOHNSON

Western Minnesota, c. 1890. Photographer unknown.

Nebraska, c. 1887. SOLOMON BUTCHER

In the late 1880s, a Kansas farmer wrote in his diary: "Rained a little last night. Enough to lay the dust. Corn nearly all dried up. For the life of me I don't see how the farmers will winter. No oats, No corn, No fruit, No grass, No nothing. Went to town today, I never saw as many farmers as discouraged as they are at this time. Nothing for their stock or their families, besides Tax Money."

Another Plains farmer declared: "If we hadn't give away s'much land to the railroads an' let the landsharks gobble it up . . . we wouldn't be crowded way out here . . ."

Nebraska, 1887. SOLOMON BUTCHE

IV. TRIUMPH OF THE CASH SYSTEM

By the end of the nineteenth century, American agriculture had undergone a fundamental transformation. Throughout large regions of the country, the self-sufficient, diversified farm of the past had given way to specialized, commercialized farming. The traditional husbandman who produced small surpluses and depended little upon cash income had been supplanted by the farmer who concentrated on the production of one or two staple commodities.

Industrialization and urbanization had provided farmers with expanding markets for their produce. The invention and proliferation of horse-powered and steam-powered machinery was enabling farmers to plant and harvest ever larger acreages. The rapid spread of transportation lines across the nation allowed crops to be shipped to markets thousands of miles away.

Increasingly, farming was being viewed as a business enterprise rather than merely as a means of existence. And the life of the farmer and his family was becoming ever more dependent upon the market economy and the cash system.

As early as the 1830s, growing urbanization in the Northeast had made a substantial impression upon the nature of agriculture in the region. In the immediate vicinity of burgeoning factory towns and commercial centers, farmers were concentrating their energy upon supplying local markets with fresh vegetables, fruits, and dairy products. In outlying districts, farmers had begun to specialize in the raising of beef or pork, or in the production of wool for the region's new textile industry. Farmers who participated in this commercial economy soon abandoned the old practice of home manufacture, which, in the past, had been an inseparable part of farm life. Store-bought cloth replaced homespun, and factory-made furniture and farm tools were substituted for homemade ones.

By 1840, the expanding urban centers of the Northeast were being supplied not only with produce from eastern farms, but also with produce from the West. A steady stream of western wheat, beef, pork, wool, and cheese was flowing into eastern markets. Some of this produce had been moved down the Mississippi River by steamer, then shipped up the eastern seaboard to Philadelphia, New York, Boston, and other ports. A larger portion had come by way of the Great Lakes and the Erie Canal. In the following decade, the flow of western goods would continually swell, as a network of railroad lines spread through the new states, connecting areas previously cut off from markets. In 1850 there were only 9000 miles of railroad track in the country; ten years later there were 30,000 miles.

By the middle of the century, western farmers were finding a steady market for their goods in Europe, as well as at home. Rapid industrialization in Britain and on the Continent had created huge urban populations and an increasing demand for cheap foodstuffs. In 1850, the United States exported 11 million bushels of wheat and 3 million bushels of corn. During the next decades exports would climb to ever higher levels. By 1897, wheat exports had risen to 217 million bushels and corn to 212 million. Meat exports, which had been relatively insignificant before the Civil War, amounted to $179 million by the end of the century. Like the cotton farmer of the South, the northern grain or livestock farmer had become vitally dependent upon foreign markets. In peak years, one third of the United States wheat crop was shipped abroad.

The continuing spread of railroad lines across the nation tended to encourage the growth of specialized agricultural regions. With transportation readily accessible, regional self-sufficiency was unnecessary and farmers devoted themselves to the production of those crops that would yield the highest possible profits in their particular area of the country. The production of wheat became the paramount concern throughout vast regions of the north central states and later in regions of Kansas and the Dakotas, Oklahoma and Texas. As the line of the frontier moved westward, the center of wheat production followed close behind, always gravitating to the cheap virgin lands to the west. At the same time, the nation's Corn Belt was taking shape. By the 1870s, farmers in the prairie region of the Midwest had found that their rich soil and moderately humid climate were ideally suited to the production of corn. They also found that the combination of hog production and corn growing would yield maximum profits.

All over the country, farmers were seeking out specialties that were particularly adapted to their region or locality and that promised to be most remunerative. New England farmers, unable to compete with the West in the production of meat, grain, or wool, concentrated their energy on highly perishable commodities — milk, vegetables, and fruit. Many New England dairymen gave up growing their own feed, finding it more economical to buy corn from Indiana and Iowa. The settlers who poured into Oklahoma, after the opening of the territory in 1889, soon began to grow huge quantities of cotton, knowing that their new fertile lands would far outproduce the depleted soils of the old Cotton Belt. In certain localities of California, Oregon, and Washington, growers plunged headlong into the production of hops. By 1890, two Washington counties alone were producing about 7 million pounds of hops annually.

Of course, agricultural specialization was far from universal by the end of the nineteenth century. Throughout large sections of the country general farming still predominated. And in all the major crop regions, old-fashioned diversified farmers, who grew a little of everything, were interspersed among single-crop farmers.

Nevertheless, the national trend was definitely away from general farming. Farm journals, agricultural societies, and agricultural educators all encouraged farmers to become more businesslike in their practices. It was urged that the farmer, like the manufacturer, specialize his operation and learn to keep a keen eye on the market. Rather than attempting to meet all his family's food needs as the husbandman of the past had done, the farmer was advised to direct his attention at producing one or two market crops and maximizing his cash income.

As early as the 1850s, the president of the New York Agricultural Society was enthusiastically expounding upon the great economic advantages of specialized commercial farming. Comparing old modes of farming with new, he stated: "At an early period 'production for self consumption' was the leading purpose; now no farmer would find it profitable 'to do everything within himself.' He now sells for money, and it is his interest to buy for money, every article that he cannot produce cheaper than he can buy . . . His farm does not merely afford him a subsistence; it produces capital . . . An extended cash market also enables him to simplify his processes. He can now take advantage of the principle which lies at the foundation of success in commercial and manufacturing pursuits, of 'doing one thing; doing it extensively and well.' " [1]

In 1868, the *Prairie Farmer* echoed these views, telling its readers: "The old rule that a farmer should produce all that he required . . . is part of the past. Agriculture, like all other business, is better for its subdivisions, each one growing that which is best suited to his soil, skill, climate and market, and with its proceeds purchase his other needs." [2]

In the years that followed, the inclination on the part of farm journals and agricultural educators to treat farming solely as a business enterprise would grow steadily stronger.

During the second half of the nineteenth century, American production of food and feed crops rose at an almost unbelievable rate. Corn production increased by four and a half times, hay by five times, oats and wheat by seven times.

The most crucial factor behind this phenomenal upsurge in productivity was the widespread adoption of labor-saving machinery by northern farmers. By 1850, horse-drawn reaping machines were being introduced into the major grain-growing regions of the country and horse-powered threshing machines were already in general use. However, it was the onset of the Civil War that provided the great stimulus for the mechanization of northern agriculture. With sons and hired laborers inducted into the army and grain prices on the rise, northern farmers rushed to avail themselves of the new labor-saving equipment. In 1860, there were approximately 80,000 reapers in the country; five years later there were 350,000.

After the close of the war, machinery became ever more important in northern agriculture, and improved equipment was constantly introduced. By 1880, a self-binding reaper had been perfected which not only cut the grain, but also gathered and bound the sheaves with twine. Threshing machines were also being improved and enlarged, and after 1870 they were increasingly powered by steam engines, rather than by horses. Since steam-powered threshing outfits were costly items — running from $1000 to $4000 — they were usually owned by custom threshermen who worked their way from farm to farm during the harvest season. "Combines" were also coming into use on the great wheat ranches of California and the Pacific Northwest. These ponderous machines — sometimes pulled by as many as forty horses — reaped the grain, threshed it, and bagged it, all in one simultaneous operation.

During this period, an endless procession of other new implements were coming onto the market — riding plows with multiple shares, grain drills which both planted and covered the seed, hay mowers and sulky hayrakes, two-row corn cultivators, disc and spring-tooth harrows, to name a few.

The adoption of labor-saving machinery had a profound effect upon the scale of agricultural operations in the northern states — allowing farmers vastly to increase their crop acreage. By the end of the century, a farmer employing the new machinery could plant and harvest two and a half times as much corn as his grandfather had using hand methods fifty years before. He could produce seven times as much hay and nine times as much oats. While a farmer and his son in the 1830s could plant and harvest a maximum of approximately 15 acres of wheat, by the 1890s,

two men with the aid of machinery could handle over 250 acres of wheat.

During the last decades of the century, the amount of capital that northern farmers invested in machinery continuously increased. Between 1860 and 1900, annual sales of farm equipment rose from 21 million to 101 million dollars. Much of the machinery purchased during the period was bought on credit. In their eagerness to secure equipment, many farmers went so far as to mortgage their farms or even their livestock. Such risky investments were viewed with great skepticism by more traditionally minded farmers. In a letter to the *Kansas Gazette* in 1877, one critic warned: "Farmers, beware of where you are drifting! Too much land and machinery will ruin you financially — destroy your credit at home and abroad . . . Contemplate now the situation! Our county literally covered over with machinery, and our Recorder's office fast filling up with mortgages." [3]

Whether they wished to or not, however, many farmers felt they had little choice but to go into debt in order to obtain equipment. Machinery had become an economic necessity in the new commercial agriculture, and if a man wished to compete in the market he was obliged to secure the necessary tools — even if it meant mortgaging his farm.

Historically, the American farmer, both in the North and in the South, had always been notorious for his practice of "land-skinning." Since land was abundant, fertile, and relatively cheap, the farmer had found it easier and more profitable to take up new land than to conserve the resources of the old. When agriculture was basically of a subsistence nature, soil exploitation had been limited to comparatively small pieces of land. But when new machinery enabled the farmer to enlarge his acreage and expanding markets stimulated him to greater production, the mining of the soil proceeded on a grander scale.

In the North, the wheat farmer mined his soil as thoughtlessly as the cotton farmer had in the South. In frontier regions, one wheat crop was planted after another until the natural fertility of the land gave out. Reports from the new western lands always told the same story — first a few years of stupendous yields, then a gradual decline. The great Wisconsin wheat boom was followed by the Minnesota wheat boom, then the Dakota wheat boom.

Of course, in every region there were always a few far-sighted and conscientious men who objected to this habitual soil abuse. In 1857, one Illinois farmer declared: "It is true that us western farmers have been skinning God's heritage, taking the cream off, and leaving for parts unknown, until humanity has a heavy bill against us for wasting the vital energies of mother earth." [4]

There were other men who believed that it was foolhardy to depend solely upon a single cash crop. In 1874, the editor of one Minnesota newspaper pointed out that the farmer who relied heavily upon wheat was taking a chance on weather, prices, insects, and other unpredictable factors. "Don't risk your *all* on wheat," he argued. "Raise corn and hogs, oats, barley, hay, flax, potatoes, sheep, cattle, poultry, bees, anything that is profitable so that if any one of these calamities befall you . . . you may have some other reliance to depend upon." [5]

Such advice, however, was rarely heeded until farmers began to feel the pinch in their pockets. When wheat yields finally declined to uneconomic lows, farmers would reluctantly adopt soil-building practices. Or they would sell out to another farmer and move on to the fertile virgin lands farther west.

The increasing commercialism of American agriculture during the last part of the nineteenth century reached dramatic heights in the development of the famous bonanza farms. The most well known of these mammoth wheat farms were located in the Red River Valley region separating Minnesota from North Dakota and in the Central Valley of California. The owners of these huge agricultural enterprises were often absentees — eastern capitalists or western investors who entered into farming on a speculative basis and who hired professional managers to oversee their operations.

The scale of production on these giant wheat farms was truly astounding for the time — each farm having thousands of acres under cultivation. During a peak year, one bonanza enterprise was reported to have had a total of 40,000 acres planted to wheat. The harvesting of such extensive acreages required an enormous investment in machinery. A few bonanza operators owned as many as 100 reaping machines, and 20 steam threshers.

The great bonanza farms were the object of much public attention and excitement. Countless articles about them appeared in newspapers and popular magazines. Farm machinery companies boasted in their advertisements that certain bonanza operators employed only *their* equipment. Writers emphasized the technological achievement that bonanza farming represented and the enormous profits that owners reaped. "Behold the working of this latest triumph of American genius," declared one writer in describing a bonanza harvest scene. When President Hayes, in 1878, toured one of the most famous of the Red River Valley farms, it was reported that the President "freely expressed admiration and astonishment at the magnitude of the operation." [6]

Compared with the millions of small farms that were being established during the period, the bonanza phenomenon seems relatively unimportant. Yet the significance of these great wheat farms lay not in their numbers, but in the fact that they so boldly signaled the direction in which American agriculture was moving. Through farm journals, popular literature, machin-ery advertisements, the average farmer was being presented with a striking new image of what constituted successful farming. And it was made abundantly clear that success lay in the direction of larger acreages, more equipment, and greater specialization.

During the last decades of the century, thousands of farmers and their families followed in the footsteps of the great bonanza farmers, hoping to reap small bonanzas of their own. Throughout the western states, scores of communities sprang up whose main purpose was to produce large quantities of wheat and whose existence was precariously balanced on the success or failure of this one crop.

In 1880, a Kansas farmer wrote: "Wheat is king in the county of Dickinson. It covers a larger area than any other cereal. And it excites more anxious thought from the time the seed is put into the ground till it is hauled to the elevator, than any other produce of the farm. This anxiety is not confined to the farmer alone. The mechanic, the merchant, the banker and the railroad corporations, all feel it and daily give expression to the feeling in the shape of the anxious enquiry: 'Is the wheat crop a failure this year?' " [7]

New markets at home and abroad, new railroad lines spreading across the country, new labor-saving machinery — these developments in the last half of the nineteenth century made American agriculture come alive with a burst of commercial energy.

In many regions of the West, great excitement centered around the quick profits that could be reaped from extensive wheat production. In the midst of Wisconsin's great wheat boom, one agricultural leader declared:

"The farmers are enjoying the good time . . . Fortune and plenty is vouchsafed to them all — stacks of grain crowning the ample fields of every farmer, granaries filled to overflowing, money plenty, old mortgages . . . cancelled and discharged of record . . . old store debts paid up and receipted, and the cash system triumphant."

Threshing wheat. North Dakota, c. 1880. Photographer unknown.

Waiting to unload wheat at elevator. Minnesota, 1879. OLE FLATEN

"Nothing interests the people of this community more than the price of wheat," declared a Minnesota minister in 1866.

"Men work in wheat all day when it does not rain, lounge around talking about wheat when it is wet, dream about wheat at night and I fear go to meeting Sabbath day to think about wheat."

Hallock, Minnesota, 1907. Photographer unknown.

In a letter to *The Dakota Farmer* in 1889, the wife of a wheat farmer wrote:

"There is probably no time of greater concern than at threshing. Hail, drouth, rust, smut, or mildew may claim a share of the farmer's crops . . . Not less than fifteen hungry men must be fed. If too much cooking is done, there will be waste. If not enough, harsh words will be said . . .

"Of course, the husband is worried too. Perhaps he has engaged a thresherman who has a machine which has stood out of doors all winter. As a result, it breaks here and there, belts wear out, boxings burn out and repairs must be ordered from the factory. The men must be laid off, the meat and pies in the pantry spoil, rains come to destroy the grain in the fields and the yields at threshing time are reduced. This means more debts, hardships and discouragements.

"If the crops are good, however, obligations are met, honor redeemed, happiness assured, and the home is spared another year . . ."

Nebraska, 1904
SOLOMON BUTCHER

Wheat harvest. Nebraska, 1912. LOUIS BOSTWICK

Threshing crew. Nebraska, 1910. SOLOMON BUTCHER

Harvesting 200 acres of corn. Kansas, c. 1890. REED

"An Illinois farmer can *die oftener* and *come to life and recuperate* quicker than any class of men I ever knew," wrote an observer in the 1870s. "One *good crop* and *fair prices* sets them up on their pins and makes them saucy."

Another Illinois observer reported: "There are farmers here who have planted corn on the same ground ever since they commenced farming . . . Corn — corn without manure, is their rotation. Corn is their motto from beginning to end . . . And should anyone presume to do differently he would be denounced as a book farmer, and thought to be incapable of getting a living by farming."

Nebraska, 1892. SOLOMON BUTCHER

Cotton market day. Guthrie, Oklahoma Territory, 1896. A. P. SWEARINGEN

"One American harvest," boasted a farm writer, "would buy the kingdom of Belgium, king and all."

Cotton market day. Guthrie, Oklahoma Territory, 1896. A. P. SWEARINGEN

Hop harvest. Oregon, 1903. DRAKE

"Yes, sir. I knew there was a boodle in hops," said a West Coast grower. "I've been in luck. Everybody will go into the business next year when they see hops go to a dollar, and they'll overstock the market and bust the price. But I'm going to get the cream of it now . . ."

Hop harvest. Oregon, c. 1900. Photographer unknown.

"Farming for a business, not for a living — this is the *motif* of the New Farmer," proclaimed an agricultural writer at the turn of the century. "He is a commercialist . . . He works as hard as the Old Farmer did, but in a higher way. He uses the four M's — Mind, Money, Machinery, and Muscle; but as little of the latter as possible."

According to this enthusiastic writer, machinery was the key to the new agriculture. "The enterprise of these Western farmers," he wrote, "brought in the present era of farm machinery. It replaced the man with the hoe by the man with the self-binder and steel plow and steam thresher. It wiped out the old-time drudge of the soil from American farms, and put in his stead the new farmer, the business farmer, who works for a good living and a profit, and not for a bare existence . . .
"American farmers are using very nearly a billion dollars worth of labor-saving machinery. The whole level of farm life has been raised . . . The use of machinery has created leisure and capital . . . The farmer of today lives in a new world."

Combines at work
Washington wheat fields, c. 19??
Photographer unknow?

Washington, c. 1900. Photographer unknown.

Threshing wheat. Minnesota, 1908. Photographer unknown.

Threshing wheat. Antelope, Montana, 1915. OLSON BROTHERS

In 1903, one farm spokesman announced, "What the farmer
wants to produce is not crops, but money."

V. A BARE HARD LIVING

For a large segment of American farmers, specialized, commercial agriculture failed to bring prosperity. On the contrary, dependence upon cash crops and the fluctuating prices of international markets brought increasing insecurity, hardship, and indebtedness.

During the last decade of the nineteenth century and the early decades of the twentieth, mortgage indebtedness rose sharply and there was a dramatic growth in the amount of farm tenancy in the country. By the end of the 1920s, a large percentage of the nation's farmers no longer owned the land they worked. Tenancy rates were exceptionally high in the specialized cash-crop areas of the country. In the eastern and western cotton belts, over two thirds of all farmers were tenants; in the tobacco region, almost one-half were tenants, and in the wheat and corn belts, approximately two-fifths.

The Great Depression of the 1930s found American agriculture in a highly unstable condition — a large portion of the farm population having only a precarious foothold on the land.

In the crisis of falling prices, many farm families would lose even this unsteady hold. The continuing advance of mechanization allowed landlords in the South to replace many of their sharecroppers and tenants with tractors. The government's crop-reduction program also encouraged the displacement of tenants in the South. Drought and dust storms added to the distress of farm families on the Plains. By the end of the 1930s, half a million farm families, mostly tenants, had been forced off the land. A million more were barely hanging on — many living in hopeless poverty.

The growth of farm tenancy in the United States had a number of historical roots. In the South, sharecropping and tenancy were to a large extent an outgrowth of the slave plantation. In the Corn Belt, tenancy rose rapidly as land values climbed, and many men, unable to purchase farms, were forced to remain renters all their lives.

Throughout the country, farm foreclosure was a primary factor in the spread of tenancy. In periods of depression, great numbers of heavily mortgaged farmers lost their land to creditors and became tenants. During the depression of the 1890s, many wheat and corn farmers in the North and small cotton farmers in the South were foreclosed, and tenancy rates in these regions climbed swiftly. In Oklahoma Territory the growth in tenancy during this period was almost unbelievable. Although the territory was only opened to settlement in 1889, by 1900 forty percent of Oklahoma farmers no longer owned their land.

The collapse in prices following the boom years of World War I saw another wave of foreclosures and another upsurge in tenancy. Often farmers who had been foreclosed remained as renters upon the land that they had previously owned.

Wherever the system of tenancy took hold in the United States, community life suffered. Whether in the North or in the South, the system was conducive to social instability, poor farming practices, and widespread discontent. In the country as a whole, two forms of tenancy predominated. By far the largest number of tenants in the nation were share-tenants — men who owned their own work animals and farm tools and who paid their landlords approximately one third of their cash crop as rent. In the South, another form of tenancy was common. In this region 40 percent of all tenants were propertyless sharecroppers, who depended on their landlords to furnish the necessary tools and stock and who paid as rent fully one half of the cotton or tobacco that they produced.

Both types of tenancy greatly encouraged a single cash-crop pattern of agriculture. Since rent consisted in a portion of the tenant's production, landlords constantly pressed for an enlargement in the cash-crop acreage. Throughout the wheat and corn belts, landlords required tenants to pay an extra cash rental for keeping land in pasture in order to graze stock. In the South, tenants and croppers were often actively discouraged from wasting their time on vegetable gardens and livestock-raising. In Oklahoma, some landlords stipulated that all good land should be planted to cotton. If the tenant wished to have a fertile garden spot, he was charged extra. Such practices caused many tenants — particularly in the South — to rely heavily upon store-bought food. Much of this food was purchased on credit, with country merchants charging extortionate rates of interest.

By tradition, tenant contracts were made for a period of one year only, and tenants were given no assurance that their leases would be renewed. Short-term arrangements of this sort did much to promote dissatisfaction and habitual mobility — approximately one third of all tenants in the country moved each year. In general tenants had only the most transitory interest in the land that they worked, and when a renter left a farm, it was usually in worse condition than when he had arrived.

In 1915, a government commission investigating tenancy in Oklahoma and Texas reported: "Where tenancy exists under such conditions as are prevalent in the Southwest, its increase can be regarded only as a menace to the Nation . . . Under this system tenants as a class earn only a bare living through the work of themselves and their entire families. Few of the tenants ever succeed in laying by a surplus. On the contrary, their experiences are so discouraging that they seldom remain on the same farm for more than a year, and they move from one farm to the next, in the constant hope of being able to better their condition. Without the labor of the entire family the tenant farmer is helpless. As a result, not only is his wife prematurely broken down, but the children remain uneducated and without the hope of any condition better than that of their parents. The tenants having no interest in the results beyond the crops of a single year, the soil is being rapidly exhausted and the conditions, therefore, tend to become steadily worse. Even at present a very large proportion of the tenants' families are insufficiently clothed, badly housed, and underfed . . . Over 80 per cent of the tenants are regularly in debt to the stores from which they secure their supplies, and pay exorbitantly for this credit. The average rate of interest on store credit is conservatively put at 20 per cent and in many cases ranges as high as 60 per cent.'' [1]

The Great Depression of the 1930s hit some American farmers with far more severity than others. Many farmers who owned their land, stock, and equipment outright managed to get through the lean years with relative ease. However, for farmers deeply in debt the Depression meant disaster. Between 1930 and 1934, more than three quarters of a million farms in the United States were foreclosed or transferred to creditors, and many more were sold to avoid foreclosure. For many tenants and sharecroppers, the economic depression also brought great hardship. The collapse in commodity prices meant that at harvest time a tenant's share of the crop was often totally absorbed in paying his store debts. As a result, large numbers of families were left without money to purchase food and clothing to get them through the winter.

In the decade of the 1930s, it has been estimated that one out of every four tenants received some form of relief, and there were many more who desperately needed help and failed to receive it. For many tenant and sharecropper families, hunger and fear became the central facts of life.

The government's crop-reduction program substantially contributed to the hardship faced by southern sharecroppers and tenants during the thirties. In order to alleviate the nation's massive overproduction problem and thereby, hopefully, raise commodity prices, the government under the Agricultural Adjustment Act of 1933 initiated a program of paying farmers for curtailing their acreage in certain staple crops. Cotton acreage was cut back by approximately one-third; other crops by lesser amounts.

The cotton-reduction program led southern landlords to evict great numbers of sharecroppers and tenants. Technically, landlords who were receiving government benefit payments were not permitted to evict their tenants. However, the Department of Agriculture in the early years of the program made little attempt to halt the process of displacement. The acreage reduction program had been designed principally to aid the upper third of the nation's farmers, and the welfare of sharecroppers and tenants had been largely ignored.

The insecurity of families living on the land during the 1930s was augmented by the rapid deterioration of the land itself. By the Depression decade, almost every section of the continent which had come under the plow was showing signs of abuse. In many areas of the country, land that only a generation before had comfortably supported a family had deteriorated to the point where it would no longer do so.

Years of overcropping and careless farming had left a deep impression on the countryside. Not only was the land being exhausted of its fertility, in many regions much of the topsoil itself had been stripped away. Throughout most of the country it was rainwater run-off that was carrying away the topsoil. On hillside farms, many fields were scarred with gullies and rills down which topsoil washed after every rain. Even on the gently sloping or almost level lands of the Midwest, huge quantities of rich prairie soil were being washed away by the slow, almost imperceptible process of sheet erosion.

Although water erosion was responsible for most of the soil damage in the country, it was wind erosion that would make the headlines during the 1930s. The great dust storms that tore across the western Plains during those years dramatically announced to the nation that the country's topsoil — the very basis of its agricultural wealth — was being swept away.

The dust storms of the thirties had been in the making for many years. During the three previous decades ever greater tracts of wild pastureland in the semiarid region of the Plains had been ripped up with gang plows and sown to wheat. Lured on by the promotional literature of land companies, railroads, and state governments, increasing numbers of farmers had moved out into the dry country. Between 1914 and 1929, at least 20 million acres of virgin grasslands were planted to wheat.

Whether the market was good or bad, farmers on the Plains tended to devote a large portion of their land to grain. During the boom times of World War I, large acreages were planted in order to cash in on the skyrocketing prices. When prices plummeted, farmers still planted extensive acreages in a desperate attempt to meet mortgage payments and stay afloat. There were many men on the Plains who recognized the danger they were running in plowing up so much land. Yet burdened with debt and harassed by landlords, most felt that they had no alternative but to take the risk.

Throughout most of the twenties, nature had been kind and the rains had fallen. Then in 1930 came the first of a series of severe and protracted droughts. No longer was there a protective cover of tough wild grasses to hold the soil in place, and when the winds blew in those years, the parched earth crumbled to dust and rose in dark clouds. From the heart of the "dust bowl" in the southern Plains all the way north to the Dakotas, the powdered topsoil was churned and borne aloft. In 1933, '34, '35, and '36, vast dust clouds moved across the eastern half of the continent, sometimes reaching as far as the Atlantic seaboard. Behind, on the Plains, millions of acres of once fertile cropland were transformed into virtual deserts.

Some of the farmers in stricken areas stuck it out, clinging to the hope that when the rains returned the land would make good once again. Many others, bankrupt and beaten, gave up the struggle and abandoned their farms to the winds and the shifting dust.

Low prices and drought, soil erosion and the government's crop-reduction program all combined in the 1930s to make the lives of millions of farm families fearfully precarious. For many tenants and sharecroppers the increasing adoption of the gasoline-powered tractor posed a still further threat.

The collapse of cotton prices, together with the perfection of the all-purpose tractor, induced many southern landlords to try to cut production costs by substituting power machinery for a large part of their labor force. During the 1930s, the number of tractors in the country doubled, and at the end of the decade one government report asserted that "nearly every one of these tractors has pushed a few tenants, sharecroppers, or hired hands out of jobs." [2]

In the Mississippi Delta region, many large cotton plantations became mechanized during the Depression years. In this plantation area, where croppers worked small plots of twelve to twenty acres, the purchase of a tractor enabled a plantation owner to dispense with the labor of at least six or eight families. Throughout the Delta, thousands of evicted black sharecroppers drifted to nearby towns where they lived much of the year on relief. During the harvest season when huge crews of pickers were needed in the cotton fields, these displaced croppers were trucked out to the plantations to work as hired day laborers.

Tractors were also displacing large numbers of tenants in Texas and Oklahoma. In this western cotton region, tenant farmers were typically whites who owned their own teams and tools and generally worked farms of 160 acres. When landlords in this region purchased tractors, they frequently threw two such farms together, evicted the tenant families, and employed a hired man to run the tractor.

In 1939, one government relief official, writing from a county in northwestern Texas, reported: "Land owners are buying tractors and renting one or two farms to work beside their own. From one to five families are being moved from farms as landowners take the land over. It is estimated that . . . 50% of the tenants have been displaced in the past six years." [3]

Another government official stated: "Today the fate of the Indian and the buffalo is in store for the small farmers of Texas and Oklahoma, if the tendency for large farms to gobble up the small ones is not stopped." [4]

Many tenant families who had been "tractored off" the land in this western cotton belt lingered in the area, getting by on relief and day labor. Many others packed their belongings into jalopies and homemade trailers and hit the road, hoping to find work in the fields of Arizona and California.

In 1938, one evicted tenant farmer in Texas described his unsuccessful efforts to locate a new farm for himself and his family. He wrote: "I can count twenty-three farmers in the west half of this county that have had to leave the farms to give three men more land . . . The outlook right now is that I will move to town and sell my teams, tools, and cows. I have hunted from Childress, Texas, to Haskell, Texas, a distance of 200 miles, and the answer is the same . . . So what is the little man going to do, the one that farms from 100 to 150 acres of land?" [5]

In the years that followed, the man with little capital would find it steadily more difficult to find a place in the nation's agriculture. Machinery would continue to supplant human beings on the American landscape, and many more farmhouses would stand boarded up and vacant.

For a large segment of the nation's farmers, dependence upon cash crops and foreign markets did not bring prosperity. Instead, it brought an endless struggle to beat low prices. It brought increasing indebtedness, insecurity, and a rapid rise in farm tenancy.

In the 1890s, one Texas cotton farmer wrote: "The same old Tale of years is the Cotton Gone, the money is all gone, two. One great Discouragin fact here is so many Farmers dont own theire Farms . . .

"Every agent, pedlar, and Every profession of men is Fleecing the Farmer, and by the time the World Gets their Liveing *out* of the *Farmer* . . . we the Farmer has nothing Left, but a Bear Hard Liveing. I live in the midst of a thick Heavey populated country of Farmers 6 miles from any Town and talk Freely with them as to how much they make. And all tell me the same Hard Tale money all gone . . .

"We have a working Energetic people that would improve if they could and Farmers in these two countys is successful in Farming, We all make it but some way we cant Keepe it . . ."

Texas, 1913. LEWIS HINE

Texas, 1913. LEWIS HINE

Daughter of a cotton sharecropper. Oklahoma, 1916. LEWIS HINE

In 1910, a presidential commission investigating problems of the nation's farm population reported:

"The greatest pressure on the farmer is felt in regions of undiversified one-crop farming. Under such conditions, he is subject to great risk of crop failure; his land is soon reduced in productiveness; he usually does not raise his home supplies, and is therefore dependent on the store for his living; and his crop, being a staple and produced in enormous quantities, is subject to world prices and to speculation . . . In such regions, great discontent is likely to prevail."

Bringing in tobacco. Kentucky, 1916. LEWIS HINE

Tobacco tenant farmer and his sons. Kentucky, 1916. LEWIS HINE

Family of a tobacco tenant farmer. Kentucky, 1916. LEWIS HINE

Stripping tobacco. Kentucky, 1916. LEWIS HINE

Son of a cotton sharecropper. Oklahoma, 1916. LEWIS HINE

Plowing land for cotton. Oklahoma Territory, 1905. MARK A. CARLETON

"The 1930s — that was the time when the hope just give out," said an ex-tenant farmer. "Couldn't get nothin' for what you grew. People half-starvin'. Closest t' hell I ever been."

The Depression struck with particular severity in the great cotton- and wheat-growing regions of the United States. In the Wheat Belt, low prices were compounded with devastating drought. In the Cotton Belt, destitute tenants and sharecroppers faced the threat of being turned off the land.

In 1938, an old Arkansas farm woman described how cotton tenants in her region had been uprooted by years of low prices, by soil depletion, and by the government's crop-reduction program:

"The government reduced the acreage, and where there was enough for two big families now there's just one. Some of the landowners would rather work the cotton land themselves and get all the government money. So they cut down to what they can work themselves, and the farming people are rented out. They go to town on relief — it's a 'have-to' case. Sharecroppers are just cut out.

"Folks from this part has left for California in just the last year or so. My two grandsons — they were renters here and no more — went to California to hunt work."

Family of a cotton sharecropper. Arkansas, 1935. BEN SHAHN

Back porch of sharecropper's cabin. North Carolina, 1939. DOROTHEA LANGE

"Tain't no while to say this is the hardest year we's ever had," said a sharecropper's wife in 1938. "We've got to move somewhere this next year . . . Plenty o' land everywhere, but no house! Turner has been huntin' a place for weeks, and every night when he comes home I run to the door to hear the news. Every day it's the same tale: 'I hain't found no place yet.' . . .

"That's the way we'll be soon — tore up and a-movin'. I wish I could have me one acre that I could call mine. I'd be willin' to eat dry bread the rest o' my life if I had a place I could settle down on and nobody could tell me I had to move no more."

North Carolina, 1935. DORIS ULMANN

Missouri, 1938. DOROTHEA LANGE

House of a tenant farmer, Oklahoma, 1939. RUSSELL LEE

"We know how to farm better than we do farm," admitted a western Kansas farmer. "We simply take chances, winning in good seasons, and losing when it fails to rain, or if the wind blows out our crops."

A tenant farmer argued, "A man on such a narrow margin as I am has got to gamble on making every cent of cash he can. *I* know it's not the best way to farm, but what can I do with . . . [the landlord] breathing down my neck?"

During the World War I years and the decade that followed, over 20 million acres of wild grassland in the semiarid region of the Plains were plowed up and sown to wheat. Much of this dry land was fit only for the grazing of livestock, and the farmers who, year after year, persisted in planting it to grain were engaged in a desperate gamble with nature.

Throughout much of the twenties, the luck of these western farmers had held, and the precious rain had fallen.

Then, in the thirties, came a series of severe and protracted droughts. When the winds blew in those years, the parched earth crumbled to dust and rose in dark clouds. From Texas to the Dakotas, the overworked soil was swept aloft, and vast tracts of western cropland were transformed into virtual deserts.

Wind-eroded field with dust-filled furrows. Texas Panhandle, 1938. DOROTHEA LANGE

Cemetery and dust. Western Kansas, 1941. IRVING RUSINOW

Dust Bowl farm. Texas Panhandle, 1938. DOROTHEA LANGE

"We're through. It's worse than the papers say," said an Oklahoma farmer after the great dust storm of 1935. "We see what a mistake it was to plow up all that land, but it's too late to do anything about it."

Windmill on abandoned farm. Western Oklahoma, 1936. ARTHUR ROTHSTEIN

Texas Panhandle, 1938. DOROTHEA LANGE

"The big fellows are working their farms with tractors and day labor," reported an evicted Texas sharecropper. "The peoples is walking the road looking for places. I don't know what's going to become of this here world. This year's the worst. About 30 or 40 families, black and white, lost their places this year, right around here."

In the decade of the thirties, the number of tractors in the country almost doubled, and it was reported that nearly every one of these tractors had pushed a few tenants, sharecroppers, or hired hands out of jobs.

One Texas landlord related, "In '34 I had I reckon four renters and I didn't make anything. I bought tractors on the money the government give me and got shet o' my renters. You'll find it everywhere all over the country thataway . . . They've got their choice — California or WPA."

Georgia tenant farmer, 1936. DOROTHEA LANGE

Uprooted Oklahoma farm woman, 1937, DOROTHEA LANGE

"Here's what I think on it — the tractor's as strong against us as the drought," asserted one displaced sharecropper.

Another cropper said, "Farmin's all I ever done, all I can do, all I want to do. And I can't make a livin' at it."

Displaced Arkansas tenant, 1936. DOROTHEA LANGE

A letter to the *Dallas Farm News* in 1937 read: "Hall County now has more than 200 tractors on the farms, and shipments of new ones are received almost daily. It appears that the big landowners have gone money-mad, and, too, at the expense, misery, and suffering of the tenant farmer, his wife, and little children . . .

"We believe that there is sufficient land for all, and that the Supreme Ruler of the Universe never intended that a few should 'hog' all the land, but that all should have land upon which to live, rear their families and enjoy the blessings of home ownership and its happy surroundings."

"Tractored out" tenant farm. Texas, 1938. DOROTHEA LANGE

VI. ROOTS IN THE EARTH

Across the broad façade of an agriculture building on one of the nation's leading universities is inscribed in large letters: "TO RESCUE FOR HUMAN SOCIETY THE NATIVE VALUES OF RURAL LIFE." When these words were inscribed in the second decade of the twentieth century, it had become apparent that America was undergoing a change of enormous significance. While the number of farms in the nation was no longer increasing, the urban population was growing by leaps and bounds. It had become abundantly clear that in the future it would be the culture and habits and values of the city rather than of the country that would determine the quality of American life.

For many thoughtful men of the time, this fact was deeply troubling. Even some men who heartily applauded industrial growth and "progress" at the same time looked back uncertainly over their shoulders, fearful that something of great meaning was being left behind.

Yet what were these "native values of rural life," a modern urbanite might well ask. What exactly were these things that men were so uncertain about leaving behind?

The answer to this question has taken a multitude of different forms, for the meaning of life on the land has varied among different individuals. Yet if one talks to a score of people who have known farm life intimately, many common themes emerge.

Many people who have been raised on farms will speak about the close family ties and the unique work relationship that have characterized farm life, and many will say it is this quality of life on the land that has been most meaningful to them. As one middle-aged man, who grew up on a Wisconsin farm, expressed it, "When I was a boy, it seems like families were so much stronger. In my family we all worked together, you know. Us kids all worked. I was doing chores almost as far back as I can remember. It was like a whole little world right there — everybody working together and wanting to make things good, everybody putting in his share. It's a good feeling, knowing you've put in your share. Sometimes it kind of hurts to think of all the things you just took for granted then. I guess I never really thought much about families and such things before my own kids started growing up, and I'd be going off to the job, and the kids would be off to their friends, and we'd all be going off in different directions. There're so many things like that — things that we just took for granted." [1]

For many Americans it has been the relative independence and self-sufficiency of farm life that has been most meaningful. Such people talk about the value of working for oneself and setting one's own schedule. They emphasize the satisfaction a man and his family feel in seeing the fruits of their own labor and in being able to produce much of the food that they need. "Mostly we just got along with what we raised ourselves," said one retired Oregon farmer. "Of course almost everyone around here used to have a big garden. Every year my wife would put up a whole cellar full of beans and peas and tomatoes and peaches and all kinds of jams and pickles. She put up meat, too. We always had our own milk and eggs and chickens, and somehow it always seemed to me you just appreciated things a whole lot more when they came off your own land. Like one time my boy got a notion to put in a patch of strawberries. He was just a little fellow, and he put in those berries all by himself, and he weeded that bed every little while and kept a good lookout for slugs and sowbugs. And when they got ripe — why you never saw anybody enjoy a strawberry as much as that boy. He'd sit there eating them one by one, just thoughtful like. Because, you see, they were his. He'd grown them all himself . . . Of course we never had lots of things that people had in town. Sometimes I know my kids would think that maybe our life wasn't so good because we didn't have those things. But looking back on it, I don't know but what we didn't really live a good sight better than lots of folks do today with all their store-bought stuff. I'm not saying it was all easy. There was lots of hard work. But to me, it was good work. And it was a good life." [2]

Strong community ties and neighborliness have also been important aspects of country life for many Americans. Many people have deeply valued the intimacy and friendliness of small, relatively stable communities where families have known each other for generations. One elderly woman, who had lived her entire life in a Texas farming community, spoke of the spirit of generosity and cooperation that she had known in her childhood — both within her large extended family and within the community as a whole. "When I was a girl," she said, "there were so many aunts and uncles and cousins and second cousins and in-laws right around here — why, when we'd all have a big get-together out there in the yard, sometimes there must have been maybe fifty people. It was a pretty sight, I can tell you — that long table spread out under the shade trees with all the chicken and pies and good things, and the men talking and joking together, and the women in their summer dresses, and the children all scurrying about shouting and laughing. When you have a big family like that, people help each other out a lot. Like if you get sick, you know there will always be someone who'll come right on over and help out with things. Lots of times, I know, the older men would help out the younger fellows who wanted to try and get a start in farming. Of course, back then, it wasn't just kinfolk that helped each other out. Neighbors, too, they'd give a hand. If a man got laid up at harvest time, all the neighbors would come over and bring in his crops for him. I remember once, this woman up the road from us got awful sick while she was laying in with her last child, and my mother and another woman nearby they took turns for weeks going over there and doing the cooking and washing and cleaning and looking after the other children. Back then, a person didn't have to beg for someone to help him. Helping other folks was just the decent thing to do." [3]

Among the many things that people find important in country life, certainly the most basic is the simple fact of living close to nature. Working with the cycle of the seasons, watching the young corn shoots push up from the ground, or seeing a newborn calf struggle to its feet — the farmer and his family are brought in touch with the fundamental processes of the natural world. They are afforded the opportunity of being witnesses and participants in the miracle of life.

No doubt there have been many farmers in America who have been essentially blind to the value and beauty of their environment. Certainly there have been many who have mercilessly plundered their soil. Yet there have also been many farmers who have had a profound appreciation for the land they have worked and have taken pride in being trustees of the earth.

In 1909, one such farmer wrote to a national magazine to express his views on the condition of farm life. His name was John Bell, and he introduced himself by saying that he was not a scholar or a fancy writer. "I am," he said, "the real-thing farmer, and milk the cows and hold the plow myself." Nevertheless, John Bell found no trouble in expressing himself on the issue that concerned him most — the great neglect and abuse of the soil which he saw taking place all around him. "The soil is God's greatest material gift to man," he wrote. "All conditions, whether of mind or commerce, which invite and promote soil exhaustion are fundamentally wrong. And the individual who deliberately fails to return to the soil its fair share of the product abuses nature, cheats and degrades himself, robs his children, defrauds the future generations, and is not an intelligent, patriotic citizen. We are told 'God is in heaven,' but where is heaven? I say, God is in the soil, in the fields, where more people have found him than in any other place." [4]

This chapter, "Roots in the Earth," is about the many American farmers and their families who have truly loved the land and who have found satisfaction in living in harmony with nature.

Almost all of the photographs that appear in the chapter were made during the 1940s and 1950s — a period when there still remained a multitude of small commercial farms in the nation. However, during these years, small-scale producers and general farmers were rapidly declining in number, and within a short while they would become economically obsolete. For this reason, the photographs in this chapter not only form a portrait of a way of life, they also mark the passing of an era in American agriculture.

The generations of farm families who have been committed to their life on the land have developed a special relationship with the natural world — a relationship that has shaped their way of thinking and molded their pattern of existence.

Describing the farm where he had spent most of his life, an Oregon dairy farmer said, "If I had to tell you how I feel about my land I don't know as I could put it into words. I know this land so well, I've lived with it so long — it's like it's grown to be a part of me. It's like my own arms or legs.

"In my mind I feel my land is always wanting me, needing me. And when I go out to work, I feel that's where I want to be and where I should always ought to be . . . That's the closest I could come to telling you . . ."

Maine, 1945. KOSTI RUOHOMAA

Bringing in feed. South Dakota, 1948. JOHN VACHON

North Dakota, 1948. JOHN VACHON

Iowa, 1940. ARTHUR ROTHSTEIN

Farm pond. North Carolina, 1966. BURK UZZLE

"This earth is God's earth," said a small southern farmer.
"Yes, we work it; we care for it; we own it. But it belongs to the
Lord. That's why it smells so good and looks so fine. We come
from it, and we go to it. It's the beginning and the end."

Spring plowing. Maine, 1945. KOSTI RUOHOMAA

Utah farmer, 1941. DOROTHEA LANGE

Utah, 1953. DOROTHEA LANGE

"After you get to raising your own chickens, potatoes, and things, you don't care for the bought ones," reflected an Illinois farm woman. "When you have a little garden of your own, you think more of that than something you buy. It's your own from the start. The same as your child is your own from the start. It's a seedling and it grows with you.

"The land is like a child. Yes. And you grow with it. It's like a revolving thing. As a child you grow up with the land and it takes care of you, and then one day you plant and it grows as a child does, and you take care of it."

Utah, 1953. DOROTHEA LANGE

Utah, 1953. DOROTHEA LANGE

Digging potatoes. Iowa, 1941. DOROTHEA LANGE

Farm woman. Virginia, 1947. SOL LIBSOHN

Mowing hay. Maine, c. 1948. KOSTI RUOHOMAA

"My grandfather came to this country to make his home," related a Wisconsin farmer. "He cleared land, and he built a large house. When he was able, he bought more land, which in time would belong to my father and his brother . . .

"When I was young, I would think sometimes that maybe I would go some place else to live. But somehow I never did go, and now I'm glad I didn't.

"A man should have roots, just like a tree has roots."

Wisconsin, 1957.
E. W. COLE

Father and son. Kansas, 1946. WALLACE KIRKLAND

Husking sweet corn. Iowa, 1941. DOROTHEA LANGE

New York, 1945. SOL LIBSOHN

Recalling his childhood and his friendship with his father, an Illinois farmer said:

"I liked being around him [my dad]. It was fun learning to do things I saw him doing, to respect him and what he was doing, and I'd want to learn the job, too. Then the day came when he'd let me do something. Then in a year I'd be a little older and he'd start me in on something new . . .

"I had other friends, other kids around the country. But Dad was my best friend."

Illinois, 1955. ARCHIE LIEBERMAN

Connecticut, 1940. JACK DELANO

Washing eggs. Iowa, 1972. GEORGE GARDNER

Illinois, 1956.
CHARLES HARBUTT

Illinois, 1947. RUSSELL LEE

Onions drying. Connecticut, c. 1950. KOSTI RUOHOMAA

Maryland barn, 1940. JACK DELANO

Pennsylvania farmer, 1945. SOL LIBSOHN

A Kentucky farmer has written:
  "The real products of any year's work are the farmer's mind and the cropland itself . . . The finest growth that farmland can produce is a careful farmer."

Haycocks. Maine, 1945.
KOSTI RUOHOMAA

VII. SOMEONE ELSE'S LAND

They are always in the fields at harvest time — men, women, and children, picking the beans, peas, tomatoes, berries for the canneries and the cities. They are not farm families; the crops they harvest are not theirs. They are the nation's migrant and seasonal laborers — the farmworkers who are forever working someone else's land.

It is the large industrialized farms — particularly those specializing in fruit and vegetable production — that have become the chief employers of this labor force. In 1974, almost 60 percent of all seasonal labor was employed by only 3 percent of the nation's farms. Great segments of American agriculture have been built on the back of this work force and depend upon it for survival. The seasonal worker has enabled enormous wealth to be accumulated, but his share in that wealth has been meager.

Seasonal labor in the United States has had a long history. As early as the 1870s, California was developing the prototype of the modern industrialized, labor-intensive farm. During this period, the state's great landowners were creating enormous vineyards and orchards, hoping to amass fortunes by supplying fresh and dried fruits to the ever growing eastern markets. The huge number of workers utilized in these undertakings was over-whelmingly Chinese — energetic and industrious laborers who worked in large gangs under the direction of a "Chinese boss" or "head boy." Chinese laborers were a great boon to the California landowner. Not only were they skilled and careful laborers, they were also willing to undertake unpleasant and arduous work, and they were willing to accept living conditions and wages that white workers would reject.

In many respects these great California ranches resembled the plantations of the southern states. Both were highly commercial forms of agriculture, requiring substantial capital investment and a large labor supply. And in both cases, the labor employed was considered to be of an inferior racial stock and was looked upon as a separate caste. Yet the California landowner considered his labor system decidedly superior to the Southerner's. For while the southern planter — both before and after Emancipation — was obliged to maintain his work force the year round, the Californian employed his crew only when needed, dismissing it at the end of the season. Herein lay the genius of the system — the employer need not accept any responsibility whatsoever for his employees' subsistence between seasons. For this reason, California growers often asserted with satisfaction that Chinese labor was even more economical than the Negro labor of the South. No permanent accommodations need be provided for the Chinese. "They lived in the fields, worked as the locusts, cleared the crop and melted away."[1]

The abundance of cheap Chinese labor had made large-scale farming both possible and profitable in California. And in the years that followed, this system of farming would become even more firmly fixed upon the state, for California's capitalist growers would continually find new sources of cheap, foreign labor. When the supply of Chinese farmworkers diminished, California landowners replaced them with Japanese immigrants. When the numbers of Japanese workers, in turn, began to decline, growers availed themselves of Mexican and Filipino labor. In addition, there was always a supply of white laborers — unemployed city workers, "bummers" and "bindlestiffs" — the landless men who trudged endlessly down California's dusty roads.

While California was developing its great fruit ranches, other regions of the country were also responding to the growing demands of eastern markets and developing similar large-scale fruit and vegetable enterprises. In New Jersey, Maryland, and Massachusetts, for example, large commercial truck and berry farms were coming into operation during the last part of the nineteenth century. In some localities, extensive acreages were devoted to vegetables, while other areas specialized in the production of strawberries or cranberries.

In the early years of development, the large amount of seasonal labor employed on these farms was chiefly local — the families of nearby general farmers or townspeople who came out to work in the fields at harvest time. However, as acreages ex-panded and labor requirements increased, it became necessary for growers to look to more distant sources in order to secure their harvest crews. Soon most of the labor force on these truck and berry farms was composed of newly arrived European immigrants, a large proportion of whom were impoverished Italian families. These immigrant families were recruited in the cities and large towns of the region. Most of the Italians lived in Philadelphia throughout the winter and were brought out by the trainload to the vegetable and berry farms for the picking season, which could last up to five months. As early as the 1890s, about 2000 Italians were being transported annually in special trains from Philadelphia to the strawberry fields around Hammonton, New Jersey.

Growers recruited their workers by means of padrones. These labor contractors would go into the Italian quarter of Philadelphia and pass from house to house, painting a glowing picture of the benefits offered workers on Jersey's farms: good wages, free housing, work for the entire family.

In 1909, a field agent for the U.S. Immigration Commission offered a description of the way of life followed by these immigrant families. "In the fields . . ." he wrote, "there are a great many young married men with small families, who work patiently and persistently. Then there are women and children in swarms; old, young, and middle-aged are found in every field. In the city most of them live in narrow, rented rooms . . . often more than one family in a single room. Here . . . the adults find such work as they can to keep soul and body alive from October until May." [2]

Sugar beet production was another early agricultural industry that required a large supply of seasonal labor. In Colorado, which became the nation's principal beet-producing state, this heavy seasonal demand was first met by the importation of German-Russians — hardworking people with large families, all of whom toiled together long hours in the fields. During the first years of the twentieth century, huge numbers of these German-Russian families were brought into the state for the long work season, which extended from late spring, when the beets were blocked and thinned, to early fall when they were harvested. However, the outbreak of World War I brought to a sudden halt the immigration of European labor, and a large new source of seasonal workers had to be secured. Within a few years, the sugar beet refineries, which recruited workers for the farmers in their vicinities, were shipping in thousands of Mexicans from Texas and Mexico. And with this new, seemingly inexhaustible supply of cheap labor at its disposal, the sugar beet industry rapidly expanded.

By the 1920s, cheap Mexican labor was proving to be invaluable not only to the sugar beet grower, but also to the cotton, fruit, and vegetable growers of California, Texas, Arizona, and other western states. In the Mexican, it seemed, the western grower had at last found his ideal laborer. It was claimed that the Mexican was docile and would submit to being bossed. It was also asserted that he did not aspire to homeownership, but was content to remain a laborer. Most important, he had been seasoned by generations of poverty and would tolerate the lowest possible standard of living. The Mexican, it was stated, "will work under climactic and working conditions, such as excessive heat, dust, isolation, and temporary employment; conditions that are often too trying for white workers. He is available in numbers for the large holdings and for farms where the housing and boarding conditions cannot be ideal . . . He is not expensive labor." [3] One south Texas farmer stated bluntly, "The Mexicans are as necessary to us as the nigger to Alabama." [4]

While large growers expressed enthusiasm for cheap Mexican labor, they sometimes found that this enthusiasm was not shared by all members of their communities. There were always a few local residents who objected to the caste system they saw growing up in their communities as a result of the increasing dependence upon penniless foreign workers. Some small farmers and tenant farmers, who did their own work with the help of their families, realized that cheap labor posed a serious threat to them and that its continued availability might mean the end of small farming in their regions. Many rural merchants recognized that they would be far better off in a community composed of many small working farmers than in a community made up of a few large landowners and a group of underpaid workers. In short, there were always people who saw clearly that while cheap labor might make a few large growers wealthy, it was not necessarily in the best interests of the community as a whole.

"Migrants are the children of misfortune . . ." stated a presidential commission in 1951. "We depend on misfortune to build up our force of migratory workers and when the supply is low because there is not enough misfortune at home, we rely on misfortune abroad to replenish the supply." [5]

Throughout most of its early history, California agriculture had depended upon the misfortune and poverty of foreign nations to furnish the major portion of its supply of cheap labor. During the Great Depression of the 1930s this was no longer necessary. Now, for the first time, thousands of white American families were reduced to such desperate straits that they were willing to tolerate working conditions that growers had previously declared only impoverished aliens would bear. By the end of the decade, over 300,000 migrants had entered California, the majority coming from Oklahoma, Texas, Arkansas, and Missouri. They were displaced farmers and tenants, victims of drought, dust, low prices, and of the government's crop-reduction program. Above all, they were casualties of the great technological change that was taking place on the southern Plains. The mechanization of cotton production in the Southwest had rendered the small cotton farmer and the tenant farmer obsolete.

Like other immigrant groups before them, they came to California to find work, lured on by stories of high wages in the fields and orchards. Many hoped that in this land of plenty, they would someday be able to gain a foothold again — to rent or buy a small tract and settle down to farming for themselves once more. What they found in California was a highly industrialized agricultural economy — an economy that had been nurtured for half a century upon cheap foreign labor and that left little room for the small farmer. The migrants of the thirties would soon discover that, in the environment of California's factory farms, they had no more chance of securing land for themselves than had the masses of foreign laborers who had preceded them.

At the same time as the pattern of small farming on the southern Plains was breaking up, a similar change was occurring in the eastern Cotton Belt. In this region the old sharecropping system was being abandoned and great numbers of sharecroppers were losing their place on the land.

Many of the blacks cast off in this process moved to nearby towns and became seasonal laborers in the cotton fields of the area. Some drifted southward to find work on the large farms in the "winter garden" area of Florida. During the winter months, these Florida migrants were trucked out daily to the fields to harvest tomatoes, carrots, beans, and peas, which would be packed in refrigerated train cars and rushed to northern markets. When spring came and the winter gardens closed down, workers were assembled into labor crews and bused north to pick corn, beans, and cucumbers in the Carolinas, berries in Virginia and Maryland, then more vegetable crops in Delaware, New Jersey, and New York. Some even went as far as Maine for the potato harvest. Then in the fall they would return once more to the citrus groves and bean fields of Florida.

This annual migration up and down the Atlantic coast continues to the present time and constitutes the backbone of the eastern fruit and vegetable industry. Each year at least 50,000 people, the great majority of whom are black, "go on the season." Packed into old cars or the beat-up buses of crew leaders, they work their way up the eastern seaboard, moving from harvest to harvest, from one dingy migrant camp to another. At the end of the season they turn southward again, in most cases no richer than when they began. "Every year I go up broke, and I come back broke," said one East Coast migrant. "I don't know why I go, even." Another migrant said, "I've been ever'place, and I got noplace." [6]

Either domestically or from foreign sources, the nation's agricultural industries have always been able to secure an abundance of cheap labor, and the government's labor and immigration policies have done much to make this possible. Because of pressure from grower interests, farm laborers in the past have been systematically excluded from the protective legislation that other workers have long taken for granted — minimum-wage laws, unemployment insurance, workmen's compensation, the right of collective bargaining, even child-labor laws — and it is only in the last few years that this situation has begun to change. Whenever growers in the Southwest have felt that there was a danger of their labor costs increasing, Congress has responded to their appeals for help by allowing agricultural workers to be imported from Mexico. Under the government's bracero program, an average of 300,000 Mexican laborers were imported annually throughout the 1950s to work in the cotton, fruit and vegetable, and sugar beet industries from California to Michigan. After years of protest by domestic farmworkers, the bracero program was finally ended in 1964. But since that time, the government has continued to allow hundreds of thousands of Mexican workers to enter the United States each harvest season — some coming in as "green carders" under the government's visa program, others entering illegally by simply slipping past the intentionally undermanned border patrol. This annual inundation of Mexico's poorest citizens has hugely benefited the large growers and corporate farmers of California and the Southwest, but it has been disastrous to local Mexican-American farmworkers, for it has impeded efforts at unionization and kept farmworker wages at poverty levels.

Industrialized, labor-intensive agriculture has left a deep impression on rural society. In areas of the country in which large-scale, labor-intensive farming is prevalent, extremes of wealth and poverty live side by side. In some of the richest agricultural counties in the United States, welfare rates are three or more times higher than the national average.

One need only drive through areas of California's San Joaquin and Imperial valleys to see this contrast. Here one passes endless tracts of row crops, orchard trees, and grapevines, planted and cultivated with surgical precision — farmland that annually yields from $1500 to $8000 per acre, depending on the crop. One can drive miles through such highly productive, irrigated land without seeing a single farmhouse, for in these parts it is not unusual for an individual or a corporation to farm thousands of acres, and absenteeism is common. Yet how do the workers who bring in these fabulous harvests fare? According to Department of Agriculture statistics, the average seasonal farm laborer in the United States earned $1844 in 1974 and was able to find work a total of 110 days. It is said that conditions in California are better than average — better than in Louisiana or Texas, or even New Jersey — but the string of run-down shacks and cabins one passes on the side of the road suggest that conditions here are far from good. In these tiny houses, one realizes there are large families who are barely getting by — just barely making a living in one of the richest agricultural regions of the United States.

Farther down the road there is harvesting going on. A line of cars and a large flatbed truck are parked along the edge of a field. The workers have been picking cherry tomatoes since five o'clock in the morning and will quit in mid-afternoon, so as to beat the heat. Now groups of them are eating their lunch, squatting in the narrow strip of shade cast by the row of cars.

A young Chicano worker looks up, smiles, and says, yes, it would be all right to talk to him for a little while and to ask him a few questions.

"No, I don't mind the work," he says. "If we get them to pay us more, then I think I would like it better to do this work than to go to the city . . . But if you want to know what I think about the way things are here — about the ranches being so big — well, I guess everywhere I have ever been it has been the same. All the ranches, the land, it belongs to a few big men, and the people they own no land. It is hard for me to believe it could be different. But if I think of it, I know that is not the way it should be. I know it is something unnatural. It is a sickness of the world." [7]

In the 1870s, a wealthy California landowner testified before a state committee on immigration:

"I think the wealth of the country will be due to the advent of cheap labor . . . I would open the door and let everybody come who wants to come . . . until you get enough here to reduce the price of labor to such a point that its cheapness will stop their coming."

During the same period, a California legislative committee reported:

"To develop . . . [the state's] latent resources and vitalize all her powers, we need sound, liberal, farseeing Legislators; men who can mould and harness *all* inferior races to work out and realize her grand and glorious destiny."

Chinese laborers and foremen in the vineyards of a 55,000-acre California estate, c. 1885. Photographer unknown.

Cranberry picker. Massachusetts, 1911. LEWIS HINE

"Substantially all Italian immigrants are poor and come to the United States to better their economic condition," stated the U.S. Immigration Commission Report of 1911.

Since immigrants had no capital, the report stated, it was "impossible for the newcomer to buy land and engage in farming . . . A good many have only the hope of owning a little farm some time in the future."

Italian cranberry pickers and padrone. New Jersey, 1910. LEWIS HINE

Pickers' shacks. New Jersey, 1910. LEWIS HINE

Raspberry pickers. Maryland, 1909. LEWIS HINE

"Children make the best pickers," asserted a Maryland berry grower in 1913.

Another East Coast grower complained, "Every year they ask for improvements — they'll want beds next."

Cranberry worker. New Jersey, 1910. LEWIS HINE

Family of Russian-German sugar beet workers. Colorado, 1915. LEWIS HINE

Filipino workers, cutting lettuce. California, 1935. DOROTHEA LANGE

Migratory agricultural worker from Missouri. California, 1936. DOROTHEA LANGE

California, 1936. DOROTHEA LANGE

U.S. Highway 54, west to California. New Mexico, 1938. DOROTHEA LANGE

"None of our folks — neither side — never lived like gypsies,"
explained a migrant worker in 1935. "We ain't never owned
nothin' much, but then we ain't had to move every time a crop
was laid by neither . . . We always farmed it. Then back in 1930
things had got so doggone tough we sold off our furniture and
radio and cow and chickens and all and pulled out of Texas for
Missouri where my woman's folks is . . .

"We thought we was goin' back to Missouri to get a place to
farm it. Jennie Bell's folks had wrote and said they'd try to find
us somethin'. Well, when we got there they was all on the
County and there shore wasn't no sign of nothin' there for us . . .

"We got in a little cotton pickin' but cotton was sorry . . . and
we heard pickin' was good over in Arizona. Well, we went and
it wasn't but we got in enough to keep us eatin' off and on, and
we run into a fellow that said fruit pickin' was good out here, so
we come on to California. We been messin' along like that ever
since, pickin' hops and cotton and oranges and peas, prunin' a
little and spacin' peaches and cuttin' lettuce and workin' at one
crop and another, and then movin' on some more. We might as
well be gypsies and be done with it. When Zetilly was born we
was campin' on a picnic ground up in Washington. We'd been
up to see could we get on a homestead . . .

"Zetilly was born on the road and she died on the road. The
undertaker's is the first house she's ever been in . . ."

Migratory workers from Oklahoma. California, 1935. DOROTHEA LANGE

Waiting for work in pea fields. California, 1937. DOROTHEA LANGE

California pea fields, 1939. DOROTHEA LANGE

Migrants' camp. California, 1935. DOROTHEA LANGE

Cotton picker. California, 1938. DOROTHEA LANGE

Migrant worker.
South Carolina, 1962.
BRUCE DAVIDSON

211

"I was born in Georgia, and my daddy worked on shares," related a black migrant worker in the 1960s. "The boss man one day told us to get off the land, and fast, because he was turning to cattle, and so we left, as fast as we knew we had to leave. My daddy heard we could get work in Florida, because there are big farms there, so we went there . . .

"My daddy became sick. It broke him, you know, trying to follow the crops . . . He loved the work, picking. He never could have lasted a day in a city, sitting there like they do and getting welfare. But he got confused, moving from place to place."

Another black migrant said, "One of these trips up the road I'm going to find me a good man to work for. He's going to pay me every dime he owes me and he's going to give me a good place to sleep and eat . . .

"Heard tell of folks who went on the season and caught hold of something good someplace and stayed there . . . Trouble is, when I get up the line to the end of the road I ain't never had 'nough money to stay there. Always got to come back and start again . . .

"One of these days I'll get up the road and I'll find me some work and stay there . . . I jus' keep on movin' 'till I find what I'm lookin' for; then I ain't goin' on the season no more."

Chopping cotton.
Arkansas, 1963.
GRANT HEILMAN

Long Island, New York, 1951. EVE ARNOLD

Migrants' shack. Long Island, 1951. EVE ARNOLD

Migratory workers' bus. South Carolina, 1962. BRUCE DAVIDSON

Cotton picker. California, 1936. DOROTHEA LANGE

"We need Mexicans for their labor, for the same reason you need a mule," declared a south Texas farmer. "If they take away our Mexicans it will knock the socks off us."

Another Texas farmer stated, "We will always need someone to do the menial work."

Migrant, picking peaches. Michigan, 1970. ANDREW SACKS

Grape picker, California, 1970. PAUL FUSCO

Mexican-Americans harvesting lettuce. California, 1963. BURK UZZLE

"I don't mind to work," said a California farmworker in 1970, "but one time I don't like to do it is when they spray the chemicals or the sulfur on the vines. That day and the next day, I don't want to work because the dust, the pesticide, falls down on my face, burns my eyes, makes me sick."

A Colorado farmworker described being caught in the fields during spraying: ". . . And then I saw a black cloud, and I smelled an awful smell, it made me sick. They sprayed . . . all over us and our food and everything. My son got so sick he couldn't work anymore or go to school the next day."

Working with the "short hoe." California, 1970. PAUL FUSCO

"I'd like them to amount to something, my children," said a woman migratory worker in the 1960s. "I don't know what, but something that would help them to settle down and stop the moving, stop it for good . . . I try to tell them that I don't mean they should leave me, and I should leave them, but that maybe one day, when they're real big, and I'm too old to get down on my knees and pick those beans, maybe one day they'll be able to stop and never start again — oh, would that be good for all of us, a home we'd never, never leave."

Recalling his childhood, a California farmworker stated, "I started picking when I was eight. I couldn't do much, but every bit counts . . . I would daydream: If I were a millionaire, I would buy all these ranches and give them back to the people."

Picking peas. California, 1961. GEORGE BALLIS

VIII. SURVIVAL OF THE FIT

In the years following World War II, American agriculture's thrust toward bigness took on a new momentum. Fueled by cheap gasoline, by the new machinery and technology, and by the endless quest for greater profits, expansion surged forward — the big investors setting the ever quickening pace. With astonishing rapidity, the 60-horsepower general-purpose tractor was replaced by a new 130-horsepower model, then by a towering 235-horsepower machine with a $40,000 price tag. The single-row corn harvester gave place to combines that could handle four rows simultaneously, then eight rows. The cost of such new equipment made it economically imperative for farmers to take on more acreage. Between 1950 and 1975, the acreage of the average American farm doubled and the value of farm machinery trebled. During the same period, the number of farms in the country with gross sales of over $100,000 increased by approximately twenty times.

Those who could not keep up with the frenzied pace were shoved aside and forced to drop out. In the new agriculture that was taking shape, there was no room for the "inefficient" operator — for the man who simply wished to live on the land and work in the soil and sell enough to pay his bills. The dairyman with twenty cows was notified one day by his milk company that they would not be making pickups at his place anymore. From now on, the company trucks were stopping only at the farms of larger operators. Small-scale vegetable producers, orchardists, and general farmers found themselves underpriced and cut out of the market by supermarket chains and agribusiness corporations. In 1950, there were over 5.5 million farms in the country; by 1975, half of these farms had been consolidated out of existence. It was all part of the life-and-death struggle that one farm spokesman called "the survival of the fit." [1]

The movement in the United States toward bigger and fewer farms has received substantial assistance from government policies and programs. While Congress has appropriated hundreds of billions of dollars for American agriculture during the course of the last few decades, the primary beneficiaries of this largess have been a relatively small number of upper-bracket farmers. The interests of small-scale producers and noncommercial farmers have been given only minimal attention. The goal of public policy has been to create an expanding, industrialized, and moneymaking agriculture. Human considerations have been of little or no importance.

In the last decades, millions of farm families have been forced off the land and into the cities, but this vast exodus from the countryside has been viewed by the U.S. Department of Agriculture with complacency and indifference. In fact, some agricultural leaders and policy makers have looked upon the loss of farm population as actually beneficial. In 1960, the future Secretary of Agriculture, Earl Butz, wrote in the USDA *Yearbook*: "The declining trend in farm population is itself a sign of a strong agriculture ... We will need fewer farmers in the future, but they must be better. They will be operating on a fast track, and the race will go to the swift." [2]

Six years later, a USDA report stated, "Our rural population is becoming largely a nonfarm one. By 1980, only one rural resident in seven or eight may live on a farm. It is generally agreed that it is neither socially desirable nor economically feasible to try to arrest or even slow down this trend." [3]

In 1972, another USDA report stated: "Agricultural policy should be directed towards maintaining agriculture as a viable industry and not as a way of life. The numbers of farms or farm population size is irrelevant except as these influence performance of the agricultural industry." [4]

Views such as these have in large part shaped our national agricultural policies — policies that have seriously neglected the interests of smaller farmers and have substantially accelerated the nation's trend toward larger and fewer farms.

Of the many government programs that have contributed to this trend, without a doubt the most influential has been the government's program of agricultural research. This research has been conducted at hundreds of agricultural colleges and experiment stations maintained by federal and state governments across the country. At these numerous institutions, government researchers have expended billions of taxpayer dollars in the de-velopment of sophisticated and costly technology that has been of benefit only to the most affluent of farmers and to the nation's agribusiness corporations. The needs of the great majority of farmers have been ignored by these institutions, and virtually no money or effort has been directed toward the development of economical, small-scale technology that might help average or low-income farmers to remain on the land. With great infusions of public money, government research facilities have designed such equipment as: automated systems for the industrial production of poultry, beef, and hogs; elaborate machinery for the extensive application of fertilizers, insecticides, and herbicides; mechanical harvesters for tomatoes, peaches, nuts, citrus, grapes, and a vast assortment of other crops. Not only has this high-priced equipment completely failed to meet the needs of the majority of the nation's farmers, in many cases the development of such technology has posed a serious threat to their survival. Small farmers have found themselves unable to compete with high-powered operators using expensive equipment and the cheap fossil fuel available in the past. Medium-sized farmers have found themselves caught up in an endless rat race — sinking ever more deeply into debt in order to obtain the new machinery.

In 1969, one USDA official candidly admitted that, for the majority of farmers, government research had probably done more harm than good. He stated that many medium-sized farmers had "been on the treadmill of technological change so long that they are frustrated about the past and present, and apprehensive of the future ... They accept the new technology as a requirement for survival ... The purchase of new machinery and the adoption of new practices often force them to overcapitalize their operations, bleed their assets, and mortgage their future returns ... When we ask what agricultural research has done for this group of farmers, the answer comes back: 'Very little.' ... We have narrowed their choices to two: either get *with* the new production efficiency technology as we are developing it, or get *out* of the farming business." [5]

The tendency of the government to serve the interests of upper-class farmers at the expense of smaller operators is reflected in a wide variety of other programs and policies. Under the government's crop-subsidy programs — first adopted in the 1930s in order to hold up farm prices — the chief beneficiaries have been the nation's largest farmers. In 1967, the wealthiest 5 percent of farmers, many of them corporations, received 42 percent of the government payments. At the same time, the poorest 20 percent of farmers received only 1 percent of government payments. It could not be otherwise, for crop-subsidy payments under the government's program have been directly tied to a farmer's output. The larger the output, the larger the subsidy. In 1971, one corporate grower in California received from the federal government subsidy payments amounting to $5 million.

Federal income tax policies also have offered special advantages to farmers in the higher-income brackets. In 1966, approximately 60 percent of the nation's most affluent farmers and agribusiness corporations (those with sales of over $40,000) received substantial reductions in their income and corporate taxes. Many of these so-called "tax-loss" farmers actually paid no taxes at all. Meanwhile, farmers in lower-income brackets, unable to take advantage of tax loopholes, contributed their full share to the federal coffers.[6]

In addition, wealthy growers and corporations have, for decades, had their large labor costs subsidized through the government's refusal to establish farmworker wage standards and through the government's importation of foreign labor. Furthermore, many large-scale farmers and corporations have been allowed to reap an enormous water subsidy by engrossing great tracts of western land, irrigated by federally constructed reclamation projects.

It is clear that in the struggle for survival that has been taking place in the nation's agriculture, the "fit" have been granted substantial assistance at public expense.

Modern American agriculture prides itself above all upon its superabundant productivity and superlative efficiency. In 1975, a leading Department of Agriculture official declared: "I want to salute the world's greatest food system: A system of wondrous efficiency which is the envy of the world. A system whose innovations continue to point the way and serve as models for every other food system on our globe . . . One American farm worker today supplies enough food and fiber for 56 people . . . Agricultural output last year was twice what it was 20 years ago." [7]

In 1970, the Secretary of Agriculture stated: "Using a modern feeding system for broilers, one man can now take care of 60,000 to 75,000 chickens. One man in a modern feedlot can handle upwards of 5,000 head of cattle. One man, with a mechanical system, can operate a dairy enterprise of 50 to 60 milk cows." [8] In 1972, *The American Farmer* noted, "A new asparagus harvester can take care of 6 acres per hour, doing the work of 400 hand laborers."

The sheer output of modern American agriculture is, without question, stupendous. Yet in order to measure the true efficiency of any system of farming, it is necessary to consider inputs as well as outputs. And the inputs of American agriculture are massive.

At present, agriculture consumes more petroleum than any other of the nation's industries. Petroleum is used not only by the machines that plant, cultivate, spray, and harvest the nation's crops, but also in the production of fertilizers, insecticides, and herbicides. Additional petroleum is used in the manufacture of farm equipment, in the production of electricity used on the farm, in irrigation, transportation, and processing. Agricultural economists who have totaled up these various energy inputs of the nation's agriculture have found that when taken together, the energy that goes into making our food is actually more than the energy contained within the food itself. According to some calculations, American agriculture now expends over five calories of energy in the form of fossil fuel in order to get one calorie of food to the consumer. [9]

The Department of Agriculture tells us that, in the last twenty years, farm production has doubled. Yet it is also true that energy inputs during this period have rapidly increased. Between 1950 and 1970, the amount of fertilizer used in the production of the country's corn crop rose by eight times, the amount of insecticides by ten times, and the amount of herbicides by twenty times. One group of Cornell scientists who have painstakingly tabulated the inputs and outputs of the nation's corn crop during the last few decades have come to the conclusion that the American farmer produced corn 25 percent more efficiently in 1945 than in 1970. Rather than become more efficient, United States agriculture, according to these experts, has become increasingly inefficient. [10]

Since the end of World War II, American farmers have been consuming cheap fossil fuels as rapaciously as the pioneer farmer once exploited the cheap virgin lands of the West. Now that our petroleum reserves have begun to diminish, the true cost of our energy-intensive agriculture has begun to be felt. We have achieved our phenomenal productivity by expending our invaluable resource of nonrenewable fossil fuel. And it has become clear to many Americans that there is no more long-range future in our present energy-depleting agriculture than there was in the soil-exhausting agriculture of the pioneer.

The energy cost is far from the only cost that we have had to pay for our modern, industrialized agriculture. Scientists tell us that the fruits and vegetables that look so beautiful in the display counters at the supermarket may contain residues of toxic pesticides. We are told that the meat we buy may be contaminated with hormones, antibiotics, and a vast array of other drugs, the long-range effects of which are endlessly argued over by the environmentalists and the chemical companies. In 1974, the government's Environmental Protection Agency reported: "Virtually every American adult carries pesticide residues in his or her body fat . . . The entire population of the U.S. has some storage of these chemicals." [11]

The attempt to thoroughly industrialize the production of food in the United States has had a profound effect upon the environment. Specialization, one of the first principles of industrialization, has brought on a host of unforeseen difficulties when applied to the growing of crops and the production of livestock. For example, the raising of animals in ever larger concentrations has led to serious health problems. When livestock are raised in close confinement, any disease present can spread like wildfire among the population, affecting hundreds or thousands of animals. In addition, animals living in an artificial, stress-producing environment — such as in a broiler house or a feed lot — may be generally less healthy to begin with and more susceptible to disease.

To protect themselves against livestock epidemics of one kind or another, farmers in recent years have become increasingly dependent upon an arsenal of drugs. These drugs have been administered to animals on a daily basis, mixed with their ordinary feed. In 1971, it was estimated that between 80 and 90 percent of all beef and poultry produced in the United States was fed a diet of antibiotics and other drugs from birth to slaughter. [12] Besides these prophylactic drugs, livestock are regularly fed large quantities of hormones and other chemicals to stimulate rapid growth. On top of all this, they receive daily doses of tranquilizers to relieve the stress brought on by high-density confinement and by the other drugs that they have consumed.

Specialization in the production of crops has also met with serious difficulties. In devoting huge acreages to a single crop, rather than diversifying and rotating crops, the farmer greatly increases the danger of ruinous insect infestations and of outbreaks of plant diseases. To guard against such devastation, the farmer of course sprays his fields with pesticides. Yet far from being a cure-all, pesticides often lead to additional and unforeseen troubles. Insects and pathogens show a remarkable ability for adaptation. Within a few seasons, new, hardier varieties emerge, and the quantity of pesticide applied to the crops must be increased. Then, in a short time, increased again.

Still further pest and disease problems have been created by the growing use of herbicides. As farmers devote larger acreages to a single crop, it becomes less feasible to control weeds by mechanical cultivation. In consequence, growers have turned increasingly to the use of herbicides, which are introduced into the soil before planting, together with the fertilizer. However, as recent studies have shown, raising crops in herbicide-treated soils significantly increases the crops' susceptibility to disease and insect attack.[13] So once again, the farmer is forced to step up his pesticide offensive.

Industrialized agriculture, in large measure, has worked in direct opposition to natural, ecological patterns — patterns that, for millennia, have maintained the fertility and health of the earth's topsoil. In nature — as in traditional, diversified farming — plants and animals exist together; there is diversity and balance and continual regeneration. In modern, industrialized agriculture, on the other hand, animals have been segregated from crops, and one crop segregated from another crop. The vast mountains of manure that accumulate at feed lots and broiler houses are considered a nuisance or a useless waste and are either simply left to decay or are flushed away through costly sewage systems. Meanwhile, the hungry cropland is fed with chemical fertilizers produced in factories — fertilizers that, although greatly stimulating plant growth, at the same time kill off the nitrogen-fixing bacteria in the soil which are essential to its continued fertility.[14] While the valuable nutrients and hu-mus contained in animal manure are being thoughtlessly thrown away, our soil is being injected with chemicals that are slowly destroying its natural vitality.

The final cost that we have had to pay for our industrialized system of agriculture has been the social cost.

In the last two decades, millions of farm families have left the land for the cities and the suburbs. And with them have come millions of farmworkers and millions of small-town residents. At present, 73 percent of our population is crowded on to less than 2 percent of our land. What this has meant for the nation is more freeways, more smog, more slums, more supermarkets, more garbage dumps. It has also meant more alienated people, more tension, more noise, more hostility, more ugliness, more violence.

In the name of progress and efficiency our countryside has been turned over to machines and technology. And our population, in large part, has lost the beauty and the joys and the peace of the land.

"The era of the family farm is gone and people might as well forget it," declared a prominent agribusiness developer in 1974. "It takes risk capital to farm nowadays, and capital investment requires a profit. That's the American way. The American consumer is spoiled rotten, but that's going to change."

The publisher of an agricultural periodical stated, "It is a dark future for Mr. Average Farmer, but plenty of opportunity for the use of brains and money to achieve new high levels of production for fewer and fewer operators."

Farmland without farmhouses. Imperial Valley, California, 1973. GEORG GERSTER

Cotton harvesting. California, 1961. JOE MUNROE

Beef feedlot with capacity for over 100,000 head. Colorado, 1962. GRANT HEILMAN

233

"I started farming in 1953," recalled a California grower in the 1970s. "At that time, I had better times than I've had any year since. The first year I didn't spray at all. The next year I didn't spray at all. The third year I probably started spraying once, the next year maybe twice and it seems that it's got progressively worse till now it's almost an every two-week occurrence that they have an airplane flying over your field. And if it's not this bug it's that bug and if not that bug it's another bug . . ."

An Indiana farmer reflected, "Chemicals in farming, it's getting to be quite expensive. It seems as though we can't farm without it. They're trying to outlaw a lot of 'em, but I don't know. From my end of it, I'd hate to be without 'em. Seems as though if we didn't have chemicals, we wouldn't have crops. It seems like the bugs and the weeds would just about take care of 'em if we didn't have the chemicals. But I don't know . . . on the other end, either . . . whether it's good for our country or not."

Spraying lettuce.
California, 1968.
JOE MUNROE

*Spraying grapevines.
California, 1972.*
GENE DANIELS

Pesticide-treated orchard. California, 1971. RICHARD F. CONRAT

Caged laying hens.
Mississippi, 1971.
USDA PHOTO

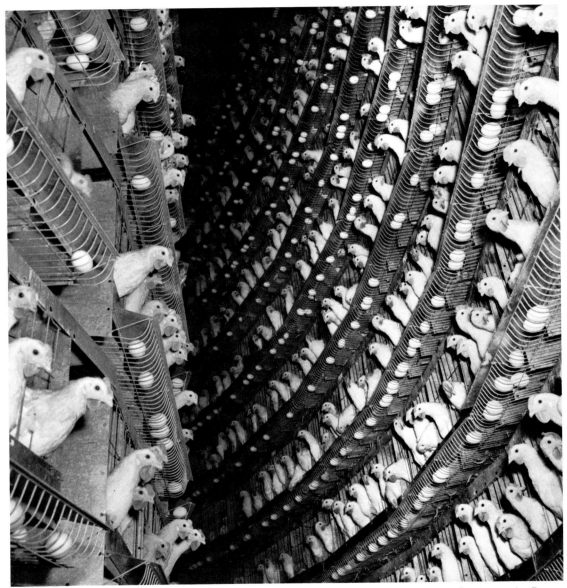

Chicken house holding 34,000 caged layers. New Mexico, 1970. © The Progressive Farmer

"We always prided ourselves on fine quality," explained a New England vegetable farmer in the 1960s. "But the supermarkets would not pay premiums. They wanted everything the same size, the same weight, and the same color and shape — nothing poor, nothing exceptional, everything good average. They don't want shoppers pawing over articles. They want the housewife to take the first thing she sees and move on . . .

"I could see that if we stayed with the chains we would have to do it their way. We would have to specialize in two or three crops and set ourselves up to trim, grade, package and wax on an assembly line. We would have to use all the tricks the chains had learned in California . . . Some vegetables will keep for weeks in plastic sheaths and still look good even though they taste like wood."

A California farmer stated, "If those damn fools in the East want my peaches at double the normal size and want my plums three inches across, okay, I'll flood my trees with water . . . so that the fruit gets good and fat and mushy. If that's what they want, that makes the living for me, okay I'll do it!"

California orchard, 1973
GEORG GERSTER

"It's a matter of survival," said a South Dakota farmer. "We can't live without this gas. If they shut off the gas, American agriculture would stop dead. We wouldn't be able to grow a potato."

Modern industrialized farming has become vitally dependent upon large inputs of fossil fuel. Petroleum is used not only by the machines that plant, spray, cultivate, and harvest the crops, but also in the production of fertilizers, pesticides, and herbicides. Additional petroleum is used in the manufacture of farm equipment, in irrigation, transportation, and processing.

In 1975, one Harvard scientist stated, "The total energy consumed by U.S. agriculture per year is equivalent to more than 30 billion gallons of gasoline. This represents more than *five times the energy content of the food produced.*"

Combines harvesting wheat.
Plane delivering machine parts.
Washington, c. 1970.
TED SPIEGEL

Montana wheat fields, 1965. KEN HEYMAN

In 1955, the future Secretary of Agriculture, Earl L. Butz, declared:

"Adapt or die; resist and perish . . . Agriculture is now big business. Too many people are trying to stay in agriculture that would do better some place else."

Harvesting wheat.
Washington, 1971.
DOUG WILSON

Abandoned farmhouse. Montana, 1969. WILLIAM A. ALLARD

Oklahoma farmer, 1946. HAROLD CORSINI

"Each year there are fewer of them," said a Maine potato farmer in 1962. "They are in debt for all they're worth. Even their crops are mortgaged before they're planted. In 1950 there were eighty-seven farmers in our town. Last year there were twenty-one . . .

"Men my age who farmed all their lives have gone to [the city] . . . They spend all they make to live in three-decker tenements."

Oklahoma, 1946. HAROLD CORSINI

In 1971, an eighty-year-old farmer reflected on the great changes that had taken place in his community during his lifetime. He said:

"These big farmers, now, they retched out and got all the land. The little guy don't get by no more."

Abandoned farmhouse. Nebraska, 1938. JOHN VACHON

NOTES TO THE TEXT

I. THE YEOMAN

NOTES:

1. William Cobbett, 1817, *A Year's Residence in the United States of America* (London: 1828), p. vi; J. Hector St. John de Crevecoeur, 1782, *Letters from an American Farmer* (New York: E. P. Dutton, 1957), p. 36.

2. Timothy Dwight, *Travels in New England and New York*, Vol. 2 (New Haven: 1821), p. 254.

3. December 20, 1787, Adrienne Koch and William Peden, eds., *The Life and Selected Writings of Thomas Jefferson* (New York: Modern Library, 1944), p. 441.

4. "Positions to be Examined Concerning National Wealth," April 4, 1769, Jared Sparks, ed., *The Works of Benjamin Franklin*, Vol. 2 (Cambridge: 1840), p. 376.

QUOTATIONS ACCOMPANYING PHOTOGRAPHS:

Page 14. "The Internal State of America," Sparks, ed., *The Works of Benjamin Franklin*, Vol. 2, pp. 462, 464-65.

Page 18. T. L. Nichols, *Forty Years of American Life* (London: 1874), pp. 6-7, 16.

Page 23. G. Hunt, ed., *The Writings of James Madison*, Vol. 6 (New York: 1900), pp. 98-99.

Page 27. John Lambert, *Travels in Lower Canada and North America*, Vol. 2 (London: 1810), p. 304.

Page 30. Letter to the Reverend James Madison, Oct. 28, 1785, Koch and Peden, eds., *The Life and Selected Writings of Thomas Jefferson*, p. 441.

II. THE PLANTATION

NOTES:

1. Barnwell Rhett of South Carolina, quoted in Carleton Beals, *American Earth* (New York: Lippincott, 1939), p. 91.

2. Joseph Holt Ingraham, *The South-West. By a Yankee*, Vol. 2 (New York: 1835), pp. 86, 91.

3. James H. Hammond, quoted in Clement Eaton, *The Mind of the Old South* (Baton Rouge: Louisiana State University Press, 1964), p. 38.

4. Speech of February 6, 1837, quoted in Richard K. Crallé, ed., *The Works of John C. Calhoun*, Vol. 2 (New York: 1851), p. 630.

5. Thomas R. Dew, president of William and Mary College, quoted in William E. Dodd, *The Cotton Kingdom* (New Haven: Yale University Press, 1920), p. 53.

6. James H. Hammond, quoted in Kenneth Stampp, *The Peculiar Institution* (New York: Alfred Knopf, 1956), p. 123.

7. Ronald Killion and Charles Waller, eds., *Slavery Time When I Was Chillun Down on Marster's Plantation; Interviews with Georgia Slaves* (Savannah: Beehive Press, 1973), p. 138.

8. *Southern Cultivator* (1849), quoted in Stampp, *The Peculiar Institution*, p. 81.

9. Norman Yetman, *Voices from Slavery* (New York: Holt, Rinehart & Winston, 1970), p. 151.

10. C. W. Howard of Georgia, quoted in M. B. Hammond, *The Cotton Industry* (New York: 1897), p. 226.

11. Governor Northern, in a 1904 speech, quoted in Rupert B. Vance, *Human Geography of the South* (Chapel Hill: University of North Carolina Press, 1935), p. 192.

QUOTATIONS ACCOMPANYING PHOTOGRAPHS:

Page 40. Senator James H. Hammond, *Congressional Globe* (March 4, 1858), pp. 962, 961.

Page 42. Quoted in David L. Cohn, *The Life and Times of King Cotton* (New York: Oxford University Press, 1956), p. 52; Ingraham, *The South-West. By a Yankee*, Vol. 2, p. 84.

Page 45. Killion and Waller, *Slavery Time When I Was Chillun Down on Marster's Plantation; Interviews with Georgia Slaves*, p. 5.

Page 48. J. S. Buckingham, *Slave States of America*, Vol. I (London: 1842), pp. 325-27.

Page 53. Quoted in Bob Adelman and Susan Hall, *Down Home; Camden, Alabama* (New York: McGraw-Hill, 1972), p. 18.

Page 55. Quoted in Rupert B. Vance, *Human Factors in Cotton Culture* (Chapel Hill: University of North Carolina Press, 1929), p. 65.

Page 59. Dorothy Scarborough, quoted in Vance, *Human Factors in Cotton Culture*, p. vi.

III. THE FARMERS' FRONTIER

NOTES:

1. Editor of the *Kansas Farmer*, in 1867, quoted in Gilbert C. Fite, *The Farmers' Frontier, 1865-1900* (New York: Holt, Rinehart & Winston, 1966), p. 14.

2. Levi Beardsley, *Reminiscences* (New York: 1852), quoted in Paul W. Gates, "Agricultural Change in New York State," *New York History*, Vol. 50 (1969), p. 132.

3. Quoted in Helene S. Zahler, *Eastern Workingmen and National Land Policy, 1829-1862* (New York: Columbia University Press, 1941), p. 130.

4. Northern Pacific Railroad broadside, reproduced in Fite, *The Farmers' Frontier*, p. 78; Kansas Pacific Railroad broadside, Land Advertisements Collection, Kansas Historical Society.

5. *Annual Report of the Commissioner of the General Land Office, 1885* (Washington: 1885), p. 79.

6. *Rocky Mountain* (Colorado) *News* (January 3, 1891), quoted in Fite, *The Farmers' Frontier*, p. 128.

7. Grant County, Kansas, settler, in letter to governor, 1889, quoted in Fite, *The Farmers' Frontier*, p. 127.

8. United States and Comanche Indian Treaty, quoted in Edwin McReynolds, *Oklahoma, A History of the Sooner State* (Norman: University of Oklahoma Press, 1954), p. 124.

9. Quoted in Fite, *The Farmers' Frontier*, p. 205.

10. Martha L. Smith, *Going to God's Country* (Boston: Christopher Publishing House, 1941), pp. 11-13, 41.

QUOTATIONS ACCOMPANYING PHOTOGRAPHS:

Page 68. Quoted in Gilbert C. Fite, *The Farmers' Frontier*, p. 15; quoted in Paul W. Gates, *Fifty Million Acres: Conflicts over Kansas Land Policy, 1854-1890* (New York: Atherton Press, 1966), p. 244.

Page 72. Quoted in Fite, *The Farmers' Frontier*, p. 13; Burlington Northern Railroad Archives, Chicago.

Page 74. From a pamphlet, Boomer Literature File, Western History Collections, University of Oklahoma; U.S. General Land Office, *Report*, 1885, p. 79.

Page 78. *The Western Shore Gazetteer* (San Francisco: 1870), pp. 201-02, in California Historical Society Library.

Page 82. From Boomer Literature File, Western History Collections, University of Oklahoma.

Page 88. *The Kansas Farmer*, Vol. 20 (December 6, 1882); quoted in Fite, *The Farmers' Frontier*, p. 129.

Page 92. Powell Moore, ed., "A Hoosier in Kansas, The Diary of Hiram H. Young, 1886-1895," *Kansas Historical Quarterly*, Vol. 14 (May 1946), p. 176; Hamlin Garland, *Jason Edwards* (New York: 1897), p. 185.

IV. TRIUMPH OF THE CASH SYSTEM

NOTES:

1. Quoted in Clarence Danhof, *Change in Agriculture: The Northern United States, 1820-1870* (Cambridge: Harvard University Press, 1969), p. 21.

2. *Prairie Farmer*, Vol. 21 (1868), p. 17, quoted in Danhof, *Change in Agriculture*, p. 22.

3. Quoted in James Malin, *Winter Wheat in the Golden Belt of Kansas* (Lawrence: University of Kansas Press, 1944), p. 73.

4. Quoted in Fred Shannon, *The Farmer's Last Frontier* (New York: Rinehart and Co., 1945), p. 169.

5. Quoted in Gilbert C. Fite, *The Farmers' Frontier, 1865-1900* (New York: Holt, Rinehart & Winston, 1966), p. 49.

6. "Dakota Wheat Fields," *Harper's New Monthly*, Vol. 60 (March 1880), p. 534; *Frank Leslie's Illustrated Newspaper*, October 19, 1878, p. 115.

7. Quoted in Malin, *Winter Wheat*, p. 99.

QUOTATIONS ACCOMPANYING PHOTOGRAPHS:

Page 102. President of the Rock County Agricultural Society, Wisconsin State Agricultural Society *Transactions for 1855*, p. 157.

Page 104. Quoted in Merrill E. Jarchow, *The Earth Brought Forth* (St Paul: Minnesota Historical Society, 1949), pp. 167, 175.

Page 106. *Dakota Farmer*, August 1889, p. 14.

Page 110. Quoted in Margaret Bogue, *Patterns from the Sod; Land Use and Tenure in the Grand Prairie* (Springfield: Illinois State Historical Library, 1959), p. 201; U.S. Patent Office, *Report* (1850), p. 199.

Page 112. Herbert N. Casson, *Romance of the Reaper* (New York: Doubleday & Co., 1908), p. 162.

Page 114. Frank Norris, *The Octopus* (New York: Doubleday & Co., 1901), Book 2, p. 58, Book 1, p. 190.

Page 116. Casson, *Romance of the Reaper*, pp. 163-64; Casson, *Cyrus Hall McCormick* (Chicago: McClurg & Co., 1909), pp. 193-94.

Page 121. Quoted in Grant McConnell, *The Decline of Agrarian Democracy* (Berkeley: University of California Press, 1953), p. 42.

V. A BARE HARD LIVING

NOTES:

1. U.S. Commission on Industrial Relations, *Final Report and Testimony*, Vol. 1 (Washington, D.C.: Government Printing Office, 1916), pp. 86-87.

2. Quoted in Broadus Mitchell, *Depression Decade, 1929-1941* (New York: Rinehart & Co., 1947), p. 220.

3. Quoted in Carey McWilliams, *Ill Fares the Land*, 2nd ed. (New York: Barnes & Noble, 1967), p. 222.

4. Farm Security Administration official, quoted in McWilliams, *Ill Fares the Land*, p. 217.

5. Quoted in Dorothea Lange and Paul S. Taylor, *An American Exodus*, 2nd ed. (New Haven: Yale University Press, 1969), p. 69; Paul S. Taylor, "Power Farming in the Cotton Belt," *Monthly Labor Review*, Vol 46 (1938), p. 607.

QUOTATIONS ACCOMPANYING PHOTOGRAPHS:

Page 130. Quoted in Norman Pollack, ed., *The Populist Mind* (Indianapolis: Bobbs-Merrill, 1967), p. 22.

Page 134. *Report of the Commission on Country Life* (Chapel Hill: University of North Carolina Press, 1944), pp. 131-32.

Page 140. Cabdriver, Washington, D.C., 1972, author's notes; quoted in Lange and Taylor, *An American Exodus*, p. 44.

Page 142. Federal Writers' Project, *These Are Our Lives* (Chapel Hill: University of North Carolina Press, 1939), pp. 20-21.

Page 146. Quoted in Carl Coke Rister, *No Man's Land* (Norman: University of Oklahoma Press, 1948), p. 175; Lois Phillips Hudson, *The Bones of Plenty* (Boston: Little, Brown & Co., 1962), p. 281.

Page 150. Quoted in Paul B. Sears, *Deserts on the March* (Norman: University of Oklahoma Press, 1959), p. 113.

Page 152. Quoted in Paul S. Taylor, "Power Farming and Labor Displacement in the Cotton Belt, 1937," *Monthly Labor Review*, Vol. 46 (April 1938), p. 855; quoted in Lange and Taylor, *An American Exodus*, p. 68.

Page 155. Quoted in Lange and Taylor, *An American Exodus*, p. 135; Federal Writers' Project, *These Are Our Lives*, p. 30.

Page 156. Quoted in Lange and Taylor, *An American Exodus*, p. 71.

VI. ROOTS IN THE EARTH

NOTES:

1. California interview, 1974, authors' notes.

2. Oregon interview, 1961, authors' notes.

3. Texas interview, 1967, authors' notes.

4. John Bell, "From the Man Who Holds the Plow," *Modern Outlook*, Vol. 91 (April 1909), pp. 826-28.

QUOTATIONS ACCOMPANYING PHOTOGRAPHS:

Page 164. Oregon interview, 1961, authors' notes.

Page 168. Texas interview, 1967, authors' notes.

Page 172. Quoted in Archie Lieberman, *Farm Boy* (New York: Harry Abrams, 1973), p. 30.

Page 176. Wisconsin interview, 1974, authors' notes.

Page 180. Lieberman, *Farm Boy*, pp. 54, 56.

Page 186. Wendell Berry, *Farming: A Hand Book* (New York: Harcourt Brace Jovanovich, 1970), p. 59.

VII. SOMEONE ELSE'S LAND

NOTES:

1. Quoted in Truman E. Moore, *The Slaves We Rent* (New York: Random House, 1965), p. 81.

2. U.S. Reports of the Immigration Commission, *Immigrants in Industries,* 61st Cong. 2nd sess. Senate Document 633, Part 24, Vol. 2 (Washington, D.C.: Government Printing Office, 1911), pp. 522-23.

3. California farm labor authority, 1930, quoted in Harry Schwartz, *Seasonal Farm Labor in the United States* (New York: Columbia University Press, 1945), p. 58.

4. Idus Gillette, Canutillo, Texas, 1927, quoted in Paul S. Taylor, "Interviews on Mexican Labor" (unpublished field notes edited by Abraham Hoffman) El Paso Valley folder, The Bancroft Library, University of California, Berkeley.

5. Report of the President's Commission on Migratory Labor, *Migratory Labor in American Agriculture* (Washington, D.C.: Government Printing Office, 1951), p. 3.

6. Quoted in Moore, *The Slaves We Rent,* p. 23.

7. San Joaquin Valley, California, interview, 1973, authors' notes.

QUOTATIONS ACCOMPANYING PHOTOGRAPHS:

Page 196. Quoted in Paul S. Taylor, "Foundations of California Rural Society," *California Historical Society Quarterly* (September 1945), pp. 207-08, 206.

Page 198. U.S. Reports of the Immigration Commission, *Recent Immigrants in Agriculture,* Part 24, Vol. 1 (Washington, D.C.: Government Printing Office, 1911), pp. 41, 103.

Page 201. Quoted in Harry M. Bremer, "Strawberry Pickers in Maryland," *Child Labor Bulletin,* Vol. 2 (1913-1914); U.S. Reports of the Immigration Commission, *Immigrants in Industries,* Part 24, Vol. 2 (Washington, D.C.: Government Printing Office, 1911), p. 530.

Page 206. Quoted in Lucretia Penny, "Peapickers' Child," *Survey Graphic,* Vol. 24 (July 1935), p. 352.

Page 212. Quoted in Robert Coles, *Migrants, Sharecroppers, Mountaineers* (Boston: Little Brown & Co., 1971), p. 424; quoted in Dale Wright, *They Harvest Despair, The Migrant Farm Worker* (Boston: Beacon Press, 1965), pp. 56-57.

Page 216. Mr. Buchanan, Big Wells, Texas, 1928, quoted in Paul S. Taylor, "Interviews on Mexican Labor," (unpublished field notes edited by Abraham Hoffman) Dimmit County folder, The Bancroft Library, University of California, Berkeley; quoted in Taylor, *Mexican Labor in the United States,* Vol. 1 (Berkeley: University of California Press, 1930), p. 370.

Page 219. Quoted in George D. Horowitz and Paul Fusco, *La Causa, The California Grape Strike* (New York: Macmillan, 1970), p. 25; quoted in Harrison Wellford, *Sowing the Wind* (New York: Grossman, 1972), p. 235.

Page 220. Quoted in Coles, *Migrants, Sharecroppers, Mountaineers,* p. 58; quoted in Studs Terkel, *Working* (New York: Avon, 1975), p. 12.

VIII. SURVIVAL OF THE FIT

NOTES:

1. Charles B. Shuman, President's Message to the American Farm Bureau Federation (Chicago, December 11, 1961), quoted in George McGovern, ed., *Agricultural Thought in the Twentieth Century* (Indianapolis: Bobbs-Merrill, 1967), p. 477.

2. Earl L. Butz, "Agribusiness in the Machine Age," USDA Yearbook for 1960, *Power to Produce* (Washington, D.C.: Government Printing Office, 1960), p. 381.

3. "A National Program of Research for Agriculture" (October 1966), quoted in Jim Hightower, *Hard Tomatoes, Hard Times* (Cambridge, Mass: Schenkman Publishing Co., 1973), p. 1.

4. "New Directions for U.S. Agricultural Policy" (1972), reprinted in *The Congressional Record,* 92nd Cong. 2nd sess. (June 21, 1972), pp. H. 5906-907.

5. Dr. Ned D. Bayley, USDA Director of Science and Education, "Agricultural Research: Arrows in the Air," speech given September 10, 1969. Reprinted in *Farmworkers in Rural America,* Hearings Before the U.S. Senate Subcommittee on Migratory Labor, 92nd Cong. 2nd sess. (June 19, 1972), Part 4-A, pp. 2150-151.

6. See U.S. Chamber of Commerce, *The Changing Structure of U.S. Agribusiness and its Contributions to the National Economy* (Washington, D.C.: Chamber of Commerce, 1974), Table 12, p. 29. This table shows that 87 percent of the lowest-income farmers reported farm profits in 1966 versus only 39 percent for the highest-income farmers.

7. Don Paarlberg, USDA Director of Agricultural Economics, in speech given in East Lansing, Michigan, July 31, 1975 (USDA 2221-75).

8. Clifford Hardin, "Foreword," USDA Yearbook for 1970, *Contours of Change* (Washington, D.C.: Government Printing Office, 1970), p. xxxiii.

9. Edward Groth III, "Increasing the Harvest," *Environment,* Vol. 17 (January–February 1975), p. 29.

10. David Pimentel et al., "Food Production and the Energy Crisis," *Science,* Series 2, Vol. 182 (November 1973), pp. 443-48.

11. Quoted in the San Francisco *Chronicle,* March 14, 1974, p. 4.

12. Harrison Wellford, *Sowing the Wind* (New York: Grossman, 1972), p. 126.

13. See I. N. Oka and David Pimentel, "Corn's Susceptibility to Corn Leaf Aphids and Common Corn Smut After Herbicide Treatment," *Environmental Entomology,* Vol. 3 (December 1974), pp. 911-15.

14. Barry Commoner, *The Closing Circle* (New York: Bantam, 1972), pp. 150-51.

QUOTATIONS ACCOMPANYING PHOTOGRAPHS:

Page 230. Malcolm McLean, quoted in *Environment Action Bulletin,* Vol. 5 (November 15, 1974), p. 1; D. Howard Doane, 1953, quoted in Wesley McCune, *Who's Behind Our Farm Policy?* (New York: Praeger, 1956), p. 163.

Page 234. Quoted in Wellford, *Sowing the Wind,* p. 239; quoted in Studs Terkel, *Working* (New York: Avon, 1975), p. 25.

Page 240. Quoted in Edward C. Higbee, *Farms and Farmers in an Urban Age* (New York: Twentieth Century Fund, 1963), p. 65; quoted in *Organic Marketing* (Emmaus, Pa.), July 1973.

Page 242. South Dakota interview, 1974, authors' notes; George Wald, "The Lethal Society," *Not Man Apart* (mid-July 1975), p. 2.

Page 246. Earl L. Butz, Undersecretary of Agriculture, addressing National Farm and Ranch Congress, Denver, *Record Stockman* (March 10, 1955), p. 1.

Page 248. Quoted in Higbee, *Farms and Farmers in an Urban Age,* pp. 57, 56.

Page 250. Quoted in Phil Garner, "Last of a Dying Breed," *Atlanta Journal and Constitution Magazine* (November 28, 1971), p. 61.

Picture Credits

(by page number)

Acknowledgments

THE PHOTOGRAPHS that comprise this book were collected by the authors during the course of several research trips made in 1972, 1973, and 1974. In all, over 100 picture collections in various parts of the country were visited, and a total of approximately 4000 photographs were gathered.

This extensive picture research, together with the lengthy job of preparing the text for the book and developing the accompanying exhibition, was made possible by grants from the Rockefeller Foundation and the National Endowment for the Humanities. The project as a whole was sponsored by the California Historical Society. We are especially indebted to Dr. J. S. Holliday, Executive Director of the Historical Society, for his years of enthusiastic and unfailing support for the project.

During our research trips, a large number of individuals at various institutions went out of their way to be helpful. They made rare and fragile collections of photographs available to us; they helped us locate the kind of pictures we were interested in; and they provided us with the highest-quality prints and copy negatives possible. We would particularly like to thank the following individuals: Alan Fern, Jerry Kearns, and LeRoy Bellamy of the Library of Congress. Daniel Lohnes of the Society for the Preservation of New England Antiquities. Madlin Futrell and John Ellington of the North Carolina Division of Archives and History. George Talbot and Chris Schelshorn of the State Historical Society of Wisconsin. James Moore, Nancy Malan, and Bill Leary of the National Archives. Sydney A. Smith of the Historic Mobile Preservation Society. Therese Heyman and Charles Lokey of the Oakland Museum. Andy Anderson of the University of Louisville Photographic Archives. Opal Jacobsen of the Nebraska State Historical Society. Jack Haley of the Western History Collection, University of Oklahoma Library. Bonnie Wilson of the Minnesota Historical Society. Howard Chapnik of Black Star. E. R. Mosteller of the Oklahoma Historical Society.

For their encouragement and advice while we were preparing the text for the book, we would like to express our deep gratitude to two outstanding authorities on American agriculture: Dr. Paul Schuster Taylor, Professor Emeritus of Economics at the University of California at Berkeley, and Dr. Paul Wallace Gates, Professor Emeritus of History at Cornell University. We would also like to thank Henry Mayer of the California Historical Society for his assistance in editing the manuscript.